The Myth of Accountability

What Don't We Know?

Eric S. Glover

ROWMAN & LITTLEFIELD EDUCATION
A division of
ROWMAN & LITTLEFIELD PUBLISHERS, INC.
Lanham • New York • Toronto • Plymouth, UK

Published by Rowman & Littlefield Education
A division of Rowman & Littlefield Publishers, Inc.
A wholly owned subsidiary of The Rowman & Littlefield Publishing Group, Inc.
4501 Forbes Boulevard, Suite 200, Lanham, Maryland 20706
www.rowman.com

10 Thornbury Road, Plymouth PL6 7PP, United Kingdom

Copyright © 2013 by Eric S. Glover

All rights reserved. No part of this book may be reproduced in any form or by any electronic or mechanical means, including information storage and retrieval systems, without written permission from the publisher, except by a reviewer who may quote passages in a review.

British Library Cataloguing in Publication Information Available

Library of Congress Cataloging-in-Publication Data

Glover, Eric S., 1947–
The myth of accountability : what don't we know? / Eric S. Glover.
p. cm.
Includes bibliographical references and index.
ISBN 978-1-61048-699-6 (cloth) — ISBN 978-1-61048-700-9 (paperback) — ISBN 978-1-61048-701-6 (electronic)
1. Teaching—Methodology. 2. Educational accountability. I. Title.
LB1025.3.G57 2013
371.14'4—dc23
2012034708

Contents

Preface		v
Introduction		1
1	Leading, Teaching, and Learning for a New Age	5
2	One Individual's Evolution	21
3	Toward Wisdom	41
4	Limiting Knowledge Limits Future	55
5	A Different Patriotism	79
6	Now Is Not Real	101
7	Seek Wisdom: Lead Inquiry	119
8	Constructing Self, Constructing Organization	135
9	Choosing to Learn	151
References		163
Index		167

Preface

As a child I never dreamed that one day I would be speaking into a microphone that would instantly translate my thoughts into written words appearing on a computer screen sitting on my lap—or that I would almost drop that computer as I reached for the still smaller computer in my pocket announcing a text message from my wife. I also never imagined teaching a class in my pajamas with African American, Hispanic, and white students sitting in front of screens at their homes in four different states.

Clearly we have made tremendous progress. We have evolved our technologies to give many of us enriched lives of convenience, comfort, and safety. We have also made great progress in evolving our social attitudes. Women have been able to vote for quite some time. We have even elected an African American president, and many states now accept gay marriage. However, we have a problem. In fact, we have a crisis looming on the American horizon.

A modern mythological beast is devouring the concept of childhood, placing limits on the future of our citizens, and denying our uniqueness as individual human beings. This monster thrives on fear. This monster not only intrudes in our technological and economic well-being, but is also encroaching on the very fabric of the social institutions that hold our nation together and enable it to move forward. However, like all mythological creatures, this modern beast was invented by humans. It is our belief in student, teacher, and school accountability. It steals our courage and leaves us recalling past successes and unable to think clearly about possible futures.

Like the imaginary giant octopi of Norse mythology that grabbed and consumed sailors daring to cross the uncharted waters of the high seas, accountability has generated a fear that is penetrating virtually every element of our society. But most importantly, its tentacles are penetrating deeply into the classrooms of the schools our children attend. These tentacles are not only reaching out to take hold of children in our most impoverished schools, but are now reaching into classrooms everywhere.

The problem is not, as most of the media report and almost all politicians argue, that our schools are failing or have failed. Indeed, most of our schools have never been better. Instead, the trouble we face is that as a society we seem to have stopped learning about who we are, from where we came, and what we may become. We were a nation burning with possibility that is becoming a nation frozen by fear. Rather than thinking about and acting upon how we can work toward a better future, we are becoming a nation accountable to the outdated practices of the past and preoccupied with losing our future to others. Rather than leading, we are trying to follow.

This mythological beast exists only in our minds. Consequently, the only way we can overcome the creature is to face it directly and squarely. This text challenges the thinking behind the fear-based policies and practices that dominate schooling in America today. I believe a better future can be secured once we overcome the flawed assumptions that support the myth of accountability. Our future success requires that we recognize our contemporary ignorance. We need to learn that we don't know what we think we know; what represents knowledge today will be tomorrow's myth.

Accountability advocates assume our children's future will be the same as our present. However, we cannot prepare children for what we do not know. Our task is to expand the range and variety of our children's knowing, skills, and ability to learn rather than limiting them to what we know now. We can't produce our children's future, but we can enable them to invent it. Each student's interests, talents, and raw abilities can be developed to create a generation with the superlative range of skills, attributes, and talents that the future will likely require but has not yet revealed.

We must also challenge the idea that reality is like a machine where each element is related to other elements in a uniform fashion. An essential element of this image is the notion of standardization. The development of standardized parts was essential for mass production and the development of the industrialized United States. Yes, standardization works well for building machines, but it is not an appropriate tool for the development of people. It is especially inappropriate for schooling America's children as we move to a complex, rapidly changing, and post-industrialized period.

Curriculum standards and regimented assessments assume that every human is virtually identical. All children, the standardization advocates say, should learn about the same thing, at about the same age, in about the same way, so that when they leave school they will each be able to do about the same thing, in the same way, at the same time. We need to remember that diversity has provided the source of our successes. Our array of differences has enabled America to become the nation burning with possibility! I suggest that our hopes for a better future are best served by staying with this quality.

Change or die is rapidly becoming our fait accompli. A primary theme of this text is that our ability to change ourselves and influence others is grounded in a unique paradox: a leader, teacher, learner relationship or *LTL* that enables an evolving social practice central to action in all successful human organizations. These ideas have value for anyone in any leadership capacity within any organization, whether that role is grounded in an official position or an informal role.

The lead-teach-learn triad or *LTL* is my description of a primary feature of human interaction providing the adaptability required for individual and group success in a rapidly changing environment. It is something I discovered as a school principal and learned from my observations of and interactions with the teachers for whom I was fortunate enough to work. This relational ability is not something most teachers consciously possess, but a natural human characteristic that our best teachers develop to a high level in spite of accountability mandates to limit it.

The text presents *developmental empowerment* and *open inquiry* as conceptual tools for understanding and practicing *LTL* in challenging our ignorance. *Developmental empowerment* is a continuum that explains how individuals construct knowledge. It presents the learner as an agent who develops responsibility rather than a worker who is accountable to a superordinate. Consequently, it represents the antithesis of the notion of accountability. *Open inquiry* is a questioning and reflective process that allows for the construction of knowledge. It is a process for influencing change in self and others.

Together open inquiry and developmental empowerment allow for the operation of the *LTL* paradox. These ideas are my representations of how we have accidentally and unknowingly constructed our thinking and actions to change America into the dynamic scientific, technological, and socially evolving nation that we have become. They enable the United States to continue as a nation becoming rather than a nation stalled, but we must come to understand this evolutionary process so that we may maintain and even expand it.

I will argue that *LTL* practice is the core idea behind contemporary learning organization and learning community theories. It is an ancient practice found in families and corporations and it is the central practice of teachers in our best schools. *LTL* is most jeopardized by the growth of standardization and accountability over the past thirty-five years. These policies are products of fear. They limit our ability as an evolving species to adapt with our environment of accelerating change. Consequently, accountability is a guarantee of failure.

I hope this text will affirm, assist, and encourage educators: teachers, principals, and others engaged in preparing our young for an unknown future. It interrogates the limits imposed by contemporary education policies and the thinking behind them. It provides an avenue for challenging these policies and identifies processes for constructing ourselves so that we can develop the leading, teaching, and learning structures that will address our present and future needs as individuals and groups.

ACKNOWLEDGMENTS

Portions of chapter 2 were modified from Glover, E. (September 2007). Real Principals Listen. *Educational Leadership* 65 (1): 60–63.

Portions of the section "Who Speaks? Who Listens?" in chapter 7 are modified from an article first published as Glover, E. (September/October 2011). Foster Change through Open Inquiry. *Principal*, web exclusive available online at www.naesp.org/SeptOct11.

Introduction

We live in a time of great change. Even the rate of change seems to be accelerating. Consequently, it is a time of great confusion. For anyone in a school leadership position, this confusion can be overwhelming. Actually, anyone in any leadership position is likely overwhelmed. Many ideas from the past that stand for representations of present truth are being contradicted and disproven. *The Myth of Accountability* is designed to provide a new way of thinking: an alternative interpretation of what is true, what is real, and what is not, so that we may adapt our thinking to our evolving environments.

This text is divided into nine chapters. Chapter 1 is a synopsis of the major ideas and themes developed in the text. This chapter challenges the limits of modern thinking associating the machine as the appropriate representation of reality and the factory as the ideal organization for human enterprise. It introduces *LTL*, the lead, teach, learn triad as the ancient and paradoxical framework that has allowed humans to become the dominant species on earth. Contained within *LTL* are developmental empowerment and open inquiry, the tools that enable us to practice *LTL* as an evolutionary process that will guide leaders through the changes we are experiencing.

The second chapter describes my personal evolution from a modern thinking, cage rattling, and knowing principal into an evolving, constructive minded, democratic leader who approaches leadership as a learner. I stopped believing in the myth of accountability and the inviolability of the machine; I discovered that the only thing I can really change is myself and that my ability to lead is connected to being as authentic as possible. Modern managers replaced the princes who ruled during the middle ages. However, leaders have influenced, always.

The philosophical backbone of the text is presented in chapter 3. It is grounded in the notion that learning occurs as a product of challenging self and others to recognize our personal ignorance. In so doing, we are able to seek wisdom. Wisdom is presented as an elusive state that is just beyond our ability to know. We can never be wise, but its pursuit has always been the essence of human progress. Our hope for the future, as individuals and a species, lies in our continuous evolution toward wisdom. That is, our future depends upon learning.

Chapter 4 initiates the challenge to the myth of accountability. Scientific ideas about the nature of complex organizations and requisite variety as essential elements of successful systems are applied to examine the accountability myth. I discuss in depth the nature of the misfit between human motivation and market ideas. I also frame the leadership shortcomings of economic and political organizations and the wrongful blaming of schools for the failures of these other institutions. Chapter 6 extends this challenge to include modern assumptions about the nature of knowledge and time. The accountability advocates are in a thinking Neverland assuming to know the future needs of children.

The successful qualities of our good schools are validated in chapter 5. The work of organizational theorists is borrowed to argue that our best schools are the real learning organizations that businesses strive to become or claim to be. The conclusion is that while not all schools are good schools, I have never been to a school that does not contain at least some of the characteristics of a learning organization. These characteristics are better catalysts for school improvement than accountability mandates that actually limit the potential for change.

Chapter 7 focuses specifically on *open inquiry* as the tool for leading the conversations required to improve schools or other organizations. It also presents the flaws in one of the most recent accountability-myth–based efforts attempting to provide machine/factory fixes to improve school quality. The focus of that section is "First to the Top," the Tennessee version of President Obama's "Race to the Top" legislation. The essential flaw of these efforts is the idea that by using accountability, a quantitative system can improve quality. Quite simply, more cannot become better.

The subject of chapter 8 is that human responsibility is an attribute that is superior to accountability. This subject is analyzed in reference to developmental empowerment as a theoretical framework for analyzing levels of personal development. The conclusion is that modern accountability systems limit the development of the individual to the lower levels of the developmental empowerment continuum, thereby limiting the development of responsibility and learning.

Chapter 9, the final chapter, addresses the ageless nature of the *LTL* triad as the communication device enabling the successful evolution of humans. It concludes that courageously acting to recognize and face our ignorance is the beginning of learning and the first choice toward becoming a responsible agent. All leaders are teachers, all teachers are learners, and all learners are leaders.

Accepting the false security of the myth of accountability is failing to make this choice. Seeking safety from our fears by believing in this myth has created a dangerous irony. The accountability beast has labeled school success as failure. While it is true that our schools can be better, as can all institutions, our real education problem is not that education is failing. Our limited thinking is failing our children. Accountability is a myth that is devouring childhood, delimiting futures, and denying humanity. Limiting our thinking led us to create this monster. Challenging our thinking, individually and collectively, is the only way to overcome it.

Chapter One

Leading, Teaching, and Learning for a New Age

> There are thinkers who claim that, if the modern age began with the discovery of America, it also ended in America. This is said to have occurred in the year 1969, when America sent the first men to the moon. From this historical moment, a new age in the life of humanity can be dated. —Vaclav Havel, President of the Czech Republic in a speech at Independence Hall, Philadelphia, Pennsylvania, July 4, 1994.

President Havel called this new age of human life the postmodern period. He said that the beginning of this new age presents a growing abyss between the "rational and the spiritual, the external and the internal, the objective and the subjective" and that we are living in a time of transition when "something is on the way out and something else is painfully being born. It is as if something were crumbling, decaying and exhausting itself, while something else, still indistinct were arising from the rubble" (Havel, 1994).

Modernity achieved great advances for humans. It was responsible for the development of science and incredibly complicated technologies. This was possible because of modern thinking that viewed the machine as the metaphor for reality. Science and technology replaced belief in the myth and magic that had previously served as solutions to human problems. However, Havel understood that our continued application of modern thinking poses dire threats for our future in this postmodern world. Indeed, our absolute belief in contemporary knowledge is the source of the abyss Havel described. Today's truth will be tomorrow's myth.

One primary tenet of the modern period was the standardization of parts that allowed for mass production. The factory became the ideal metaphor for organizing people to accomplish work. The assembly line was a machine of humans. Each human cog in this machine completed one or more standardized tasks and passed the incomplete object on to another worker in a standardized sequence until the product was complete. This text proposes rethinking the relationship between people and the way they participate in organizations.

It is time to understand that reality is not merely a giant complicated machine that operates on a sequence of steps that can be described as one-way, cause-effect relationships. There is much more to human organization than what is visible on an assembly line. Indeed, even in the few factories remaining in America, most of the interactions of the workers go unnoticed except by the participants themselves. They do much more than simply complete assigned tasks. These folks are engaged as complex living people with their work and one another. Although it is seldom recognized, these human interactions actually keep the assembly line operating.

This text challenges the accountability systems associated with standardization as elements of the modern period. Standardization and accountability are declining as ideas in service to humans. Accountability is standardization applied to humans. It is control placed upon a worker by someone higher in an organizational hierarchy. It takes form as external rewards and punishments designed to motivate toward a desired end. Ideal accountable workers are not expected to be morally and ethically responsible. They are expected only to complete assigned tasks. In the modern thinking framework, moral-ethical frames come from higher levels.

This text challenges modern thinking by focusing on schools. It questions the thinking that chooses to make accountability a central feature of efforts to improve the learning of children. Modernity has always viewed teachers as workers who are accountable only for completing the tasks prescribed by organizational hierarchy. Modern school strategies define human learning as elements easily measured by standardized systems. Education policies are increasingly focused on examining teacher work, and attaching carrots and sticks to standardized measures. Unfortunately, increasing accountability diminishes teacher ability.

Most teachers do not view their work as simply responding to the external demands placed upon them by a higher authority in the organization. They tacitly know that the young humans they serve are more than data storage systems that can be accessed by standardized measurements. Most teachers see themselves as more than merely accountable workers. They are agents who accept responsibility for enabling our young people to develop the skills and abilities that will enable them to live successful lives.

The machine was the metaphor for reality and the factory for the ideal human organization of the modern world. In the postmodern period, these metaphors will become learning and the school. Success for our children will depend upon developing the knowledge, skills, and abilities that go beyond the acquisition of easily measured standardized information. Students will need the adaptability to challenge contemporary knowledge and create new understandings in a world of accelerating change. School success will be more dependent on the development of individual teacher and student responsibility than on accountability.

It has been twenty-five years since the publication of *A Nation at Risk* (National Commission on Excellence in Education, 1983) labeled our schools as failing systems and generated an ongoing fertile field for political exploitation. Chapter 4 will conclude that this report was wrong in its analysis of the *education problem* and wrong in the outcomes it predicted. In fact, that report was a gross misrepresentation of what was happening in American schools.

However, that report did get one thing right: Education is the core issue we must work through for a better tomorrow. Unfortunately, the solutions advocated by the Reagan White House and repeatedly attempted by subsequent administrations have moved education practice in exactly the wrong direction. The purpose of this text is to present a new direction. It questions the modern mechanical paradigm, seeking a deeper understanding, and a wiser approach for our future.

An ancient and common human attribute is identified in this text as *LTL* or the lead-teach-learn triad. The leadership process evolved by humans is most evident in mother-child relationships and teacher-student interactions. *LTL* is the leadership practice commonly found in good schools and behind much of the success enjoyed by Americans. It is the foundation upon which human cultures and societies have developed and the natural human characteristic common to all good teachers. Additionally, although often hidden, it is found in all successful organizations. Unfortunately, it is denied by modern accountability thinking and practice.

LTL is the sophisticated human quality that makes humans uniquely different from other living creatures. It is exhibited whenever two or more individuals are in a relationship with one serving as leader and the other as learner. *LTL* is common practice among good teachers. Indeed, the author came to understand the power of this attribute while serving as a school principal who learned to value and trust the tacit wisdom of good teachers (Glover, 2007). He learned to build upon teachers' strengths and support their work rather than trying to fix teachers as policy makers, regulators, and central administration expected.

KNOWERS ARE NOT LEARNERS

The philosophical hallmark of the modern period is empirical positivism. It provided the thinking framework that enabled modern thinkers to reject the myth and magic that served to guide human behavior from ancient times through the Middle Ages, replacing it with the logic of cause-effect relationships symbolized by the machine representation of reality. Now it is time for another thinking change. The machine image of reality is contemporary myth.

Empirical positive thinking guided humans to create the modern state, develop scientific objectivism, and generate the economic engines of industrial-age capitalism, as well as the failed totalitarian systems of fascism, Nazism, and communism. It has also served as the guide for the development of schools patterned as factories. Modern schools treat students as if they are raw materials modified to achieve predetermined notions of what it means to be educated. Teachers are treated as factory workers who complete these predetermined tasks, supervised by principals serving as line operators.

Unfortunately, *LTL* practices in schools are increasingly threatened by modern machine age thinking manifested through contemporary education policies and practices. In giving us curriculum-based standards and standardized testing, modern thinking limits what teachers teach and what students learn. These limits are based upon the false assumptions made by policy makers, curriculum developers, and standardized test developers. These folks come to their work believing they know what each child will need to know for a successful future and where that child is in her or his learning journey.

Indeed, modern organization theory fails to recognize that learning begins with the recognition of personal ignorance. Most organizational thinkers, authorities, and practitioners start their theorizing and perform their work with the assumption that they have the knowledge needed to guide the organization to success. They simply do not understand that their knowing is limited in time and space. When the organization does not respond to their expert direction, these knowing actors find fault with their failing subordinates. Then they assume that the subordinates, like parts in any machine, need to be fixed or replaced.

Although the *LTL* concept was generated for this text, it represents the primary tool available for understanding the limits of modern ideas. It is an interpretation of the unique and exquisite social characteristics that define humans as a species. *LTL* is commonly found in families, communities, companies, and countries. The *LTL* theme is developed through the text to reach the conclusions presented in chapter 9. The interactive communication ability labeled *LTL* represents the adaptive tool that for thousands of years has enabled humans to grow our knowledge and survive.

A paradox of human existence is that we cannot be wise, but our future depends upon seeking wisdom. Hidden within the lead, teach, learn concept is the idea that a knower cannot learn. In other words, practicing *LTL* as an individual and a member of a group is seeking wisdom, an elusive state that is beyond knowledge. It is an ancient inquiry process that begins with individual recognition of a state of ignorance—a need to know.

Most elected officials and policy regulators have based their decisions on the idea of a failed or broken school system. We commonly hear them say that the schools need fixing. However, failing schools are merely a symptom of the real problem. Those with organizational power and authority are trapped by the knowledge that limits their thinking to machine-age solutions. It is time to realize that the blind belief in the power of objective, cause-effect tools to solve all problems cannot work.

Of course, education is *the* central problem of our time and will continue to be so for a long time. How could it be otherwise? This is a time of rapid acceleration in the rates of technological and social change. Consequently, it should be no surprise that the way we prepare our young for an unknown future should be a primary concern. Unfortunately, our society, stuck in modern thinking, is failing to help, encourage, and in many places, even allow our educators to develop effective schooling practices for this new human period.

Rather than blaming teachers for failing to achieve externally mandated *fixes* that actually contribute to the problems they are designed to address, we should be celebrating the successes that teachers achieve in spite of the external mandates that contribute to the problems they are designed to fix. Indeed, we need to elevate the status of teaching. Enabling our young to develop the attributes needed for an unknown future requires much more than providing them with the factoids necessary for passing a standardized test. Teaching must become a professional career. It requires professional agents rather than accountable workers.

LTL: THE LEAD-TEACH-LEARN TRIAD

The elements required for real school success are contained in the unique, paradoxical, and ancient *LTL* relationship. Teaching is leading, leaders must learn, and only learners can teach. This complex human communication capability is the core element of quality schooling and the characteristic of social evolution most threatened by our continued application of the mechanical thinking and practices common to modern organizations. This text incorporates the naturally evolved leading, teaching, learning triad or *LTL* into a formal thinking, acting, and understanding framework for challenging the limits imposed by modern organizations.

The *LTL* relational framework developed for examining how we think about ourselves, how we relate to one another, and how we experience change. Embedded in the lead-teach-learn triad are *open inquiry* and *developmental empowerment*. *Open inquiry*, the subject of chapter 7, is a set of question processes for engaging organizational participants to think deeply about their goals and the actions they take to achieve them. It is a necessary tool for changing ourselves and our organizations. Chapter 8 addresses *developmental empowerment*, a constructivist view of human self-understanding that represents our purpose for leading, teaching, and learning.

LTL is a newly invented concept but a very old practice. It is a process that we can perhaps first observe when a child looks into her or his mother's eyes and she responds. *LTL* is the common but very special natural interactive ability that has enabled humans to evolve into the creatures that dominate the planet. Confucius, Solomon, Jesus, Mohammed, Gandhi, and Martin Luther King were all leaders and teachers who generated learning that changed the world.

However, although *LTL* has been with us all along, it is a quality that we have ignored in the modern period. The lead-teach-learn triad is the common relational feature that has always been abundant in successful schools and the quality that enables those schools to be successful. *LTL* is the set of practices and relationships at the heart of any organization that learns. You can most likely think of a teacher or teachers from your own schooling or elsewhere in your life who helped you to change. If so, then you have experienced *LTL*.

LTL contains one other quality that distinguishes it from modern thinking. This is the recognition of the frailty of knowledge. Knowledge is limited because it is a human representation of some portion of reality. We can validate the limits of knowledge by tracking its evolution through history. Indeed, changes in human knowledge parallel the evolution of humans and our civilizations.

Consequently, this text resurfaces the ancient notion of wisdom as an elusive or even impossible state to achieve. Seeking wisdom requires that we recognize that knowledge is limited because it continuously evolves: today's knowledge is tomorrow's myth. Recognizing that we don't know what we think we know generates a discomfort that requires questions. Questioning is the teaching mechanism that allows us to recognize our ignorance and the thinking place where learning begins. It is seeking wisdom and the source of successful human social and technical evolution.

BLAME, FIX, BLAME: A VICIOUS CYCLE

The machine metaphor represents reality in the modern world and the factory is the organizational vision of that metaphor. Schools were designed to be copies of the modern factory with specific outcomes planned as system products. Students were the raw materials moved through the factory beginning with grade 1. According to this design, they were sorted by teachers and principals to their appropriate levels in society and manufactured into workers.

Children of immigrants were stamped with the English language and white middle-class values. Children who fit definitions of high intellectual ability based upon white middle-class values were encouraged to stay in school and rewarded for their intellectual prowess. With luck, children perceived as less intellectually capable were assigned to career-technical programs. Those not quite as lucky were encouraged by the design of the system to drop out of school and find employment in factories. This system worked very well in modern America. Plenty of factory jobs were available that paid a living wage.

Recently, that sorting assignment has changed. Now, our world and our schools are in transition. Today, most of those factory jobs have moved overseas and schools have been given a postmodern goal. They are assigned the task of generating success for every student. This is certainly a wonderful goal, and hopefully one that can be achieved; but this is a new goal for schools.

Unfortunately, proposed solutions for addressing the growing abyss between this laudable goal and the realities of schooling are exacerbated by our outdated machine-age definition of success and the application of mechanical solutions. Our understanding of education systems is stuck in a modern paradigm. This thinking prevents us from developing the necessary political policies and processes needed to support our postmodern education goal. In order to develop these essential changes, we must evolve our thinking.

Ever since Ronald Reagan was in the White House, we have wrongly faulted our schools for much of what is wrong in America. Today the ongoing assignment is for the educator to "reform," "change," and "improve" according to externally designed mechanical devices. However, the issues that parents, teachers, and principals face are complex and deeply seated in the structure of our society. Contemporary mechanical accountability systems cannot address deep structural complexity.

In spite of decades of blame by politicians, our schools are not liable for the flaws of society. The opposite is more truthful. Our schools are responsible for much of the success we have had and continue to have in our country. What is described as school failure is the misplaced assignment of blame for symptoms of the larger social maladies of economic and social injustice. Consequently, our schools, our teachers, and most importantly, our students are often the victims of misguided policies and practices that do more harm than good.

Yes, many of our schools in areas of high poverty, serving high concentrations of poor and minority children, have not overcome the barriers society has created for them—barriers that continue to grow. However, the United States has multiple systems of education that include some of the best and worst schools in the world. Overall, our schools are providing the majority of young people in the United States with a continually improving education. It is true that the improvements have not kept up with the rate of technical and social change, but this is not only an American problem. No country on the planet is keeping up.

The real problem of American education is not low test scores. The real problem is defining all schools as the problem, blaming all educators for that problem, and generating complicated mechanical solutions for complex social issues. Many, perhaps most educators and other people who care about our schools share these feelings, but often do so covertly. School bashing has become the fashion du jour. Consequently, it is quite risky to speak out in support of what our schools are accomplishing.

Essentially, policy makers and compliant practitioners act as though they can know, predict, and control the future. These policy makers and the education practitioners who advocate their policies are trapped in the modern, empirical, positivist-thinking framework. According to the modern positivist, we can solve the education problem by doing what seems to have worked in the past—but doing it more and calling it better.

These modern folks believe we can *fix* the education machine and the school factory with more regulation and greater standardization. What modern-thinking policy makers say we need are firmer controls for teachers, principals, and schools. Those punishments and incentives that the policy makers and regulators build into the system will guarantee success, or so they believe and promise.

However, the gap between what has changed and what needs to change continues to grow. The modern, positivist thinker looks for cause-effect relationships, unable to see the complexity beyond. The positivist theorizes that an input into a system should yield a specific output. If the solution has not fixed the problem, then something or someone must be at fault. Therefore, depending on with whom one speaks, the fault lies with parents, teachers, school administrators, unions, school boards, liberals, conservatives, or . . .

Now this blame syndrome has reached a new level. Just about everyone in the public sphere seems to agree that if we can just fix the schools we will fix just about everything, including the economy and our political standing in the world. The common retort is that, "We will be able to compete globally!"

But the perception of failing schools is not *the education problem*. It is a symptom of the real problem: the limits of modern, mechanical thinking. Simply applying solutions available only within that thinking framework compounds *the problem*.

This is what we are experiencing in our schools today. The modern positivist's understanding of *the education problem* isolates it to a problem of schooling and attempts to *fix* schools. However, it is more than a school problem. It is the universal need to enhance the ability of individuals and groups to evolve our learning so that we are more able to adapt ourselves and the systems we generate in a time of accelerating change. The *education problem* is really a complex issue that universally affects individuals and organizations: schools, communities, companies, and our nation.

A common cliché is that we must learn to learn. Just about everyone says this, but few people try to understand it or do it. It requires a continuous examination of what we individually and collectively know, and an understanding of the limits of our knowing. This is an increasingly important issue and one our schools don't address well. However, our schools continue to address our need to learn better than other institutions, in spite of modern education policies that limit their ability to do so.

HUMANS ARE COMPLEX

Lead, Teach, Learn identifies the set of thinking processes and action practices that enhance our individual and collective ability to learn, adapt, and change ourselves and one another. *LTL* is complex. Consequently, this text is not a set of blueprint directions or a step-by-step plan. An automobile is the product of such a set of complicated plans. It is complicated because it contains thousands of parts that fit together in exactly one way: it is a machine—a modern, standardized, mechanical system.

Most automobiles have been duplicated thousands of times and each unit is virtually identical, so that when parts break they can be replaced by a nearly exact replica that will work just as well as the original. However, without that replacement part the car fails to function and ceases to exist as a machine, becoming a pile of useless parts. You have likely driven by many junkyards full of former cars that have become piles of rusting parts.

Like the automobile, our current education policies and the practices that emanate from these policies are mechanical and increasingly complicated. We have more standards, more testing, more specific procedures than ever before and have been continually adding to these policies and procedures for many years. The results of these policies and practices actually reduce real positive change in the quality of education afforded our children.

These policies and practices are actually symptoms of the thinking that has created and continues to create those problems. We are trapped in a vicious cycle where the selling of the lie of declining test scores continues to result in more testing and increasing regulatory measures in the name of accountability that result in additional testing and regulation. Our efforts to do more of the same while adding more complicated parts and labeling them as different, have not worked. Echoing Albert Einstein, doing the same thing repeatedly and expecting different results is insane.

Rather than creating and enforcing increasingly complicated mechanical policies that interfere with teaching and learning, can we turn in a new direction and build upon the complexity and democratic qualities that have provided the strength of our society and the core of American schooling? The strength of our society and schools has more to do with freedom and experimentation than with control.

Indeed, the education problem is not that our schools have not changed. They have. The problem is that the evolution of our technology and as a consequence our social structures are accelerating at a rate faster than our schools are changing. But contemporary education policies limit the adaptability of schools. Most education policies actually inhibit change and experimentation at the very time they are most needed.

Teaching is the characteristic that has enabled humans to elevate our status among all creatures. We humans are just better teachers. Leading and learning are the two required identifiable elements under the umbrella of teaching. Leading is the process of generating change in followers, and learning is the realization that change is possible. Teachers are the leaders who facilitate the realization of possible futures. Learners choose to follow. We are all followers and we can all be leaders.

Generally, in classrooms the followers are students—but not always. The teacher is an investigator who must follow the leads provided by the student. Learning for the teacher involves discovering the needs, wants, interests, and thinking frames of the student and relating specific content and ideas to that individual. It is reflective and involves the teacher discovering herself or himself as a learner and leader. Another cliché we often hear is lead, follow, or get out of the way. A leader-teacher-learner must do all three simultaneously and expand her or his capacity for so doing, within the context of specific situations.

The label assigned for this complex relationship is the lead-teach-learn triad or *LTL*. Learning for students and/or followers is seeing and discovering their own possibilities. In discovering their unique possibilities they are also leading the teacher to understand where and how capacity and ability fit for each of them. Obviously, the lead-teach-learn relationship can be complicated, but it is always complex. It is an ongoing collaborative process of discovery by the teacher and the student as leader and learner.

DEVELOPMENTAL EMPOWERMENT AND OPEN INQUIRY

Human development is grounded in our ability to communicate. Consequently, modern dialogue theory, including the works of Belenky, Bond, and Weinstock (1997), Bohm (1996), Ellinor and Gerard (1999), Isaacs (1999a; 1999b), and others, has been incorporated to support the work of building on human strength and complexity as contributors to seeking wisdom in schooling and generating an understanding of the *LTL* framework. Two related contextual frames have been developed as tools for helping us build upon human potential. They are *developmental empowerment* and *open inquiry*.

Developmental empowerment or *DE* examines the developmental levels of an individual's understanding of relationships with others. It is based upon the work of Belenky, Bond, and Weinstock (1997), who engaged economically poor women in dialogue groups and assessed the growth that occurred in the women's thinking processes. The work of Belenky et al. is grounded in feminism, specifically in the development of individual voice and an ethic of care.

A parallel relationship exists between these women in traditional roles within their communities and the placement of teachers and teaching in our society. These disempowered women were without a voice, and teaching is a profession with, at best, a very limited voice. Consequently the Belenky et al. framework has been adapted to describe the intellectual growth of teachers and principals and labeled *developmental empowerment*.

Open inquiry or *OI* is a set of leadership practices that can surface authentic voice, thereby generating and releasing organizational participant energy to challenge barriers that interfere with success. Some refer to this participant energy as *ownership*. Principals and superintendents often speak of wanting teachers to feel ownership for whatever new program has been adopted in a district. However, ownership is a property right: an economic term that is not an appropriate representation for human beliefs.

We all experience ownership. Property can be bought and sold. But most education policies and the politicians who crafted them speak of accountability. Both ownership and accountability are tied to market ideas and related to the exchange of goods and services. However, owners are not accountable to others. Instead, others are accountable to owners. If teachers are accountable for some aspect of their work, they simply cannot own it.

Accountability and ownership are modern economic inventions. Responsibility is a unique human characteristic that has evolved over thousands of years. It is tied to an ethic of care (Gilligan, 1982), and a more appropriate term for belief-based human effort. Responsibility is a dedication to a high level of care for others. The prime example is that the parent is responsible for the health and well-being of the child. Responsibility is also an attribute of every good professional in any field: an airline pilot is responsible for the safety of passengers, a doctor for care of patients, and a teacher for the learning and well-being of children or younger adults.

This is not the same as the ownership that an entrepreneur feels for the enterprise in which she or he engages. The entrepreneur has an ownership right to her or his property. The owner may also be well satisfied with the accountable performance of her or his employees. However, entrepreneurs and their employees can and often do demonstrate great responsibility for the organization's workers and customers. They too can exhibit responsibility that goes beyond the market-based notion of accountability. The point is that property is owned and those who work for an owner are accountable whether or not they are responsible.

Accountability is limited to the tasks assigned to the employee by the owner. Responsibility is a human attribute related to social, moral, and ethical relationships. It is the umbrella of care for which the *T* stands in the lead-teach-learn or *LTL* triad. *Developmental empowerment* provides a purposeful way for school leaders (teachers, principals, superintendents, and others) to think responsibly about self and others. *Open inquiry* provides a set of practices that can assist them in achieving that purpose in unity: it challenges participants to think and learn together.

THE MISSING PIECE OF THE SCHOOL CHANGE PUZZLE

Just how can individual school leaders and school leadership teams go about generating and supporting the relationships that allow for the investigations into the complex and deep-seated issues that afflict our schools? Researchers and writers in the fields of educational leadership, management, and administration such as Fullan (2001), Marzano (2005), Reeves (2006), Schlechty (2002), and Sergiovanni (2008) have made valuable recommendations about change that are relevant to the needs of schools today. These authors recognize that the quality of human interaction is a core issue in working to improve teaching and learning.

Palmer (2004) focused upon the needs of educators to discover their uniqueness as individuals so that they learn to live "divided no more" (p. 9) and find encouragement in rejoining "soul and role" (p. 10). Lambert (2003) has provided a constructivist leadership framework that focuses upon engaging teachers in conversations about teaching, learning, and problem solving. These works prescribe what should be happening in schools.

Schlechty (2002, 2011) recognized the role of leaders as collaborative inventors of meaningful student engagement. Writing from a learning organizations perspective, Kohm and Nance (2007) provided descriptions of techniques they have developed and used for working with teachers and others in schools. Marx (2006) posed the need to focus school leadership on addressing future needs through strategic analysis of trends and possibilities. These writers and others understand the essential value of professional relationships and conversation among school participants.

These are all pieces of a puzzle that must be constructed somewhat differently in every school. Indeed, it must be constructed differently in every organization and it can be successfully constructed only by the participants of that organization and not through policy makers' efforts to control, no matter how sincere those rule-making folks may be. Complex human beings cannot be fixed by outside forces applying complicated mechanics.

What is missing in this literature is a personal view of and philosophical frame for understanding human organization tied to specific leadership practices that can serve as a foundation for change. *LTL*, the leader-teacher-learner, triad is a leadership/change process and theoretical framework that meets the needs of the individual and the group. It can serve as a guide for engaging individual educators or groups in school communities in leading their teaching and learning.

LTL is grounded in an interpretation of the pragmatic philosophy and the constructivist concepts developed by Dewey, Piaget, Vygotsky, and others. This view supports schools in moving away from the power-over practices resulting from the mechanical metaphorical frames behind standardization and accountability. These frames inherited from the scientific objectivity of modern positivism continue to dominate P–12 education policy. *LTL* builds professionalism and responsibility in P–12 teaching and leading practices.

The *LTL* leadership framework will challenge all levels of participation in organizations, as it must if the status quo is to change. But the focus of this framework is on challenging the modern thinking that leads to the limits imposed on practice by standards and accountability. It does not directly challenge people in positions of power and authority. Such efforts would likely fail and perhaps lead to ending the challenger's participation in the organization. Instead *LTL* is grounded in valuing others and self-reflection. It is a wisdom-seeking process. It can lead power and authority to self-challenge.

The focus in applying open inquiry and developmental empowerment encourages participants regardless of their power status within an organization. Any participant in any organization can examine the qualities of her or his participation and model that examination for others. Therefore, it invites participation. Most importantly, this view gets to the underlying personal and cultural issues that serve as barriers to school improvement. These are barriers that teachers, principals, parents, district administrators, and policy makers often generate without knowing that they have done so.

Inherent in this framework are the tacit practices occurring in schools and society that are examples of *LTL*. In other words, this text provides words to describe these practices, but they have long existed as a core feature of good schooling. Indeed, these practices get to the heart of human social success. They are the practices of all positive human relationships and all good organization. Chapter 5 documents the successes of our schools as representations of real-world applications of learning organization theory: a theoretical framework advocated for business organizational practice today.

Many schools in our country are learning organizations. Rather than asking our schools to mimic the modern practices of business organizations, our society would be better served if our private sector modeled the best practices of our schools. Additionally, the principals and teachers who practice within these schools are modeling what can be described as a form of patriotism: a wisdom-seeking patriotism that seeks to improve our society rather than merely approving it as it is and, by consequence, limiting what it can be.

The central message of *LTL* is found in the paradoxical relationships between leadership, teaching, and learning. It is a wisdom-seeking, postmodern, post-mechanical, post-standards process of discovery through communication; its purpose is human development. These ideas have consequences for the continued success and survival of our schools, our nation, and even the human species.

Chapter 2 traces the author's evolution as a school principal. Initially this view of the principalship was of a modern, positivist, instrumentalist who saw students and teachers as objects for whom problems are identified, analyzed, and solved. This evolved into seeing the principal as a moral leader (Sergiovanni, 2008; Fullan, 2003), a constructivist leader (Lambert, 2003), an interpretivist leader (Hall and Hord, 2006), an artist (Kelehear, 2006), and an inventor (Schlechty, 2002; 2011), who recognizes that the function of school leadership is developing the capacity of teachers and their students to generate opportunities and solutions for themselves.

QUESTION ASSUMPTIONS TO EVOLVE THINKING

The original purpose in writing this manuscript was to address the needs of principals to provide adaptive and practical leadership for the schools, students, teachers, and parents they serve. However, that purpose for leadership has expanded to include teachers, parents, and others who care about the future of people. We must all be leaders in influencing the development of a future we desire. Indeed, the only way we can have a future that we want is to all be on the design team that develops it. Perhaps this is the only way we can have a future at all.

So, described here are processes that attempt to overcome the short-sighted modern mechanical thinking that has created contemporary beliefs, policies, and practices. The focus of this text is schooling. However, the process of separating education from the rest of our endeavors is part of the dilemma we face as citizens. Contrary to a long tradition suggesting that education is above politics, modern schools are actually political policy makers' objects.

These education objects are driven to where the politicians want to go as if they were automobiles. Unfortunately, the mechanical accountability systems the politicians use to drive these cars require constant *fixing*. The focus herein is to portray schools and educators, not as objects to be manipulated, but as subjects and models for our society to emulate. The postmodern period is better driven by learning than by politics. The engagement of educators as active participants in the evaluation and development of public policy is appropriate, healthy, and essential for our future.

However, our policies and the structures that limit our futures are effectively challenged not through confrontation, but rather through questioning. This is an evolutionary rather than a revolutionary process. After all, revolution destroys and evolution creates. We must learn to question our individual beliefs and assumptions, and the beliefs and assumptions of others, so that we understand how our ways of thinking and our states of knowing limit our ability to generate the changes the future will require.

In other words, education provides the location upon which to build a process for questioning what we do in our society. Questioning provides for an examination of what we do and can demonstrate that we often unknowingly work against our collective interests and might do better. In essence, if the primary organization metaphor for modern America were the factory, in a postmodern America the symbol will need to be a school: a complex, open system of leader-teacher-learner citizens. Therefore, the author hopes that educators, parents, members of our communities, and citizens generally will find some wisdom in this old teacher's vision.

Chapter Two

One Individual's Evolution

We are all transformed by our thoughts and the leading, teaching, and learning practices in which we engage. This chapter traces the author's evolution from an individual needing to occupy a position of knowing, a position often requiring a defense, into an individual who is coming to recognize the limits of individual knowing, and, by consequence, all knowing. This has surfaced recognition of personal ignorance and a discovery of freedom and joy in learning to question. Release from the limits of modern knowing continues to be essential for the personal journey toward understanding. This chapter describes the first steps of the author's journey. Perhaps it may suggest a path for others.

SMOKEY WAS WRONG: VALUING FIRE

Many Americans grew up seeing and hearing advertisements with Smokey the Bear saying, "Only you can prevent forest fires." But at the age of fifty-six, the author was learning that the thinking behind Smokey's admonition was dangerously flawed. In 2001, hundreds of homes in Los Alamos, New Mexico, had burned and much of the surrounding country was destroyed in the Cerro Grande forest fire. This fire had been initiated as a preventative burn by rangers in Bandelier National Monument near Los Alamos. A preventative burn is an intentionally set fire designed to burn out undergrowth and prevent more serious fires.

After experiencing weeks of evacuation from the community, the students and faculty were able to return to campus for just a few days before the school year ended. As the school's principal, the author spent that time attending to the battered nerves of students, parents, and teachers. One moment stands out during those last few days of school. During lunch, a fourth-grade girl walked up and took the author's hand, and said, "Did you know my house burned down?"

The author's response was, "Yes, Melissa, I did. How are you?" She paused for a long time. During her pause, thoughts surfaced of the history of Los Alamos transitioning in the 1940s and 1950s from an elite, upper-class boys' school into the birthplace of the atomic bomb, and a premier, national scientific laboratory. Its people had built a town on Ponderosa Pine–topped plateaus and lovingly protected those forests so that they became dangerously overgrown. As Smokey had taught, we human residents knew that we are nature's stewards. Preventing forest fires was child's play compared to releasing the energy of the atom.

The school secretary and her family had stayed at the author's home while the town had been evacuated. Her home was one of those destroyed. She had bravely focused upon the comfort of her children and husband, expressing concerns about losing pictures and family heirlooms but not about losing furniture and a lovely home with a brand-new family room addition.

Finally, Melissa said, "I think we are OK." She released the author's hand, skipped to join her friends, and went outside to play. Her answer was striking. In response to the question about her as an individual, she had responded with "we." Then, she joined other children happily engaged with one another on the playground in spite of the acrid smell of burned forest still permeating the air.

Outside, a giant helicopter sent waves of vibration into the air as it flew just west of the schoolyard, carrying a giant vat of water aimed at a smoldering area high on the side of the mountain. This giant machine appeared smaller and less significant as it flew into the distance. Finally, appearing tiny, the helicopter's giant vat opened and created what appeared as a small puff of grey smoke as its contents contacted the smoldering area beneath.

That night, reflections on Melissa's statement surfaced the author's recollections of a text by Parker Palmer (1993). He quoted the words of Robert Oppenheimer, the scientist who was most responsible for the development of the atomic bomb and the development of Los Alamos National Laboratories. Eventually, Oppenheimer came to question his work. He said:

> I have felt it myself. The glitter of nuclear weapons. It is irresistible if you come to them as a scientist. To feel it's there in your hands—to release the energy that fuels the stars. To let it do your bidding. To perform these miracles—to lift a million tons of rock into the sky. It is something that gives people an illusion of illimitable power and it is, in some ways, responsible for all our troubles, I would say—this what you might call technical arrogance that overcomes people when they see what they can do with their minds. (Transcript of *The day after trinity: J. Robert Oppenheimer and the Atomic Bomb*, p.16, quoted in Palmer, 1993, p. 1)

Palmer (1993) was discussing the objective nature of our Western worldview and the way it relates to teaching and learning. Most people see themselves surrounded by objects that they view as separate. They manipulate those objects through power and coercion. Thinking only in terms of cause and effect leads to ignoring the possible connections between objects and people—between teachers and students. He said that some of the new epistemologies tell us that we should speak only of nature and ourselves at the same time.

Yet Smokey had warned, "Only you can prevent forest fires." Those commercials were produced in support of the U.S. Department of the Interior's long-standing forest fire prevention policies that had allowed the forests around the Los Alamos community to become dangerously overgrown. These policies were developed in the belief that humans are the stewards of nature and preventing fires is helpful to forests, humans who, like Oppenheimer, were guided by technical arrogance.

Unfortunately, recent experiences in Yellowstone and other areas had taught us that fire is a natural part of nature's cycle of renewal. With great pain, the people of Los Alamos were learning this as well. In believing that humans are nature's stewards, forestry experts had come to see this larger picture and created a policy for controlled burning. But even this policy revision addressed only a small part of a still larger picture. Although officials routinely checked the weather reports, no one had predicted the ferocity the wind would achieve or that these forces would continue for weeks.

Analyzing his own arrogance as a teacher and leader, Palmer wrote:

> If we believed in this organic relationship of the knower and the known, we would create a classroom practice that would teach us not to rearrange the world but to learn its intricate relationships. The knower would become a person whose destiny is not to rule, but to raise to consciousness the interrelated quality of all of life, to enter into partnership with nature, history, society, and ourselves. (Palmer, 1993; p. 38)

For many years, we humans thought we knew more than we knew as we attempted to prevent forest fires. After realizing the limits of our understanding in that regard, we believed nature could be controlled by our selective sponsoring of forest fires. Relating the events of the fire and its aftermath to Palmer's statement exposed a new understanding of reality for the author. Just as we humans cannot control nature, a principal could not drive change in school.

It was becoming clear that a principal's hopes, dreams, will, and effort could not and should not be the determining factors for the school. The future and the path to get there is much more complex than any individual's technically arrogant ability to control. Ultimately, the author would learn that the teachers, parents, community with whom he worked shared similar goals, but surfacing those goals and acting upon them is a complex process. Personal intent, effort, and will alone could not improve the school..

The author was soon to discover that the strength of a principal's position did not lie in the technical authority with which it came. Indeed, that authority often gets in the way. It is possible to be with others as we participate in ways that surface each individual's honesty, concerns, questions, ideas, and responsibility. Their questions and ideas were to become the author's as well. Creating a better future is not up to one individual alone, but as Melissa said and as the school secretary's actions confirmed, "We are OK." The teachers, parents, and students with whom the author worked could and should influence future events together.

EVOLUTION STAGE 1: LEARNING TO SEE

The author's first elementary principalship was in a small New Mexico district with approximately 600 students in grades pre-K through four. Beginning work in this school revealed a very traditional organization with norms that supported maintenance of a toxic culture (Cromwell, 2002). Several, but not all, of the teachers in this school looked at children as collections of deficits in need of repair. They simply did not know any other way of looking at students. Rules and their enforcement outranked caring relationships and support.

The previous principal's primary role had been fixing children's behavior for the teacher. Parent conferences rarely happened, and only then to address student behavior, not learning needs. Teacher professional development did not occur. One teacher explained that the school's previous principal attended conferences and meetings away from campus, but not the teachers.

Many of the teachers had become accustomed to, and liked the predictability of rules and expected the principal to do little more than enforce compliance with those rules. These teachers were frightened by expectations for staff participation in decision making and encouragement of parent involvement in the school. They enjoyed the safety provided by the repetition of their jobs, maintenance of the status quo, and barriers separating them from parents.

A new teacher, who had been a student in the school several years before, explained that she was shocked when she entered the classroom of one of her former teachers and felt as though she had stepped back in time. Her former teacher, now colleague, had changed so little. The same faded posters that had been there when that new teacher was a third-grade student still adorned the walls.

These teachers had settled on doing things in a certain way and could not perceive a different way of doing school. After all, they believed the school was successful and knew that many people in the community shared their belief. Indeed, compared to many schools in surrounding communities this school was successful. Students test scores were higher, although back then no one paid much attention to that, and the school had few discipline problems. So, several teachers asked, "Why change?"

In contrast to the expectations of these teachers were a number of new teachers and a few veteran teachers frustrated by the gaps between the educational theory they had learned in college and the expected practices of the school. They were uncomfortable with the notion that "we have always done it this way," exacerbated by some of the inequities of organizational practice in the school.

Of particular concern to these folks was the veterans' practice of collecting instructional materials before new teachers had an opportunity to do so. Of course, this left new teachers' students short of necessary textbooks and supplies. These newcomers, the veterans believed, needed to pay their dues. The veterans addressed the needs of their own students. They were not responsible for or concerned with other teachers' kids.

There had also been a long-standing tradition of parents selecting their children's teachers. Consequently, the veteran teachers actively recruited the students they wanted for their classrooms, with telephone calls and personal contacts at church and community events. New teachers were assigned the students who were not recruited, and, of course, these were the students with the greatest academic and social needs. They were also the students who provided the greatest challenges for teachers.

The results of these school traditions were that the veteran teachers' students typically performed at much higher levels than those of newer teachers. This helped maintain an aura of quality teaching for the experienced teachers, and assisted with their ongoing recruiting. As a result, students with the greatest needs often received the least support, and it was difficult for the principal to keep the best newer teachers.

Over the next six years the old culture was repeatedly challenged as the author brought many changes to the school and the district. Much to the chagrin of other principals in the district, a parent-teacher organization was created. The school board was successfully lobbied to initiate regularly scheduled parent-teacher conferences twice each year. A school advisory team labeled TEAM or Teachers Educating, Advising, and Mentoring involved several teachers in a variety of leadership roles. These changes were perceived as threatening by many of the veteran teachers in the school.

Parent and community expectations for the school were changing. Several parents who had gone away to college and returned to the community became active in the school. They aligned with the newer teachers, the veteran teachers who supported the changes, and with the author. However, the group of veteran teachers who opposed the changes had a history of being able to depose principals. One of those teachers said, "I was here before you came and I'll be here after you go." In fact, the superintendent had warned, "Be careful."

In December, the superintendent shared his initial evaluation of the author's performance. Anticipating that the superintendent would be pleased with the changes initiated in the school, the author was shocked by the written evaluation and the superintendent's words. His expectations were that 90 percent of the teachers who completed a principal evaluation questionnaire must give the principal "effective" or "very effective" ratings. Thirty-two of forty teachers had registered one of these positive ratings, but eight (20 percent) had not. In fact, four teachers had met with the superintendent to complain about the author's incompetence.

Reflecting on this first semester as principal in this school over winter break brought about an important decision. The changes in the school were good for the students and the community. The author would not focus on winning the support of those who were so critical of the changes. After all, conflict is a natural element of change. His personal view was of a heroic, challenging leader working to minimize and isolate anyone in opposition. The goal was to be a knowing, change-oriented leader, viewing other people as tools for fulfilling those purposes.

Over the next six years, an alignment of active parents, new teachers, and some experienced teachers became the "in-group" in the school. This was a win-lose political campaign: a conflict framed by two opposing belief systems played out as competition for resources and control of the school. Over time, the in-group coalition grew, gaining support and power within the school and across the district. During the author's six-year tenure as principal, numerous changes were initiated, lobbied for, and pushed through.

These changes included reorganizing Title I programs resulting in a 20 percent reduction in student–teacher ratios; enabling the development of inclusive, multi-age classrooms; arranging for parents to be trained in grant writing, resulting in funding for arts and technology programs; and creating a partnership with a local college to provide on-campus teacher education classes. Several parents and instructional assistants who went through this college program became teachers in the school, the district, and in neighboring districts as well.

Additionally, the author led the creation of a curriculum-based assessment report that discontinued letter grades. This was a precursor for standards-based grading formats. This was made possible because a parent-teacher organization and a school newsletter had been initiated. The parent organization was the only organized lobbying group and the newsletter was the single school publication in the district. In other words, the author largely controlled school communication across the district.

Most importantly, staff professional development focused on the teaching of writing. A "Writing Samples Catalogue" had been developed from collected samples of student work. Teachers compared samples of their students' writing at each grade and across grades. As a result, student scores on the New Mexico writing assessment vastly improved. The year before the writing focus, only 13 percent of students scored a median score (3.0 on a scale from 0 to 6.0) or higher. The first year, 45 percent scored a median or better score. The following year, 81 percent scored a median score or better.

As a result of these changes, the school was recognized by the Coalition of Essential Schools as an "Exemplary New Mexico School." In response to the author's testimony at a New Mexico Legislative Education Study Committee meeting, the New Mexico State Department of Education Learning Director described the school as "a beacon for New Mexico Schools."

At this point in his evolution, the author was very much a cage-rattling, mover-shaker, take-charge type of principal. Each year, the opposition "out group" became less effective in opposing the changes initiated, and the school received accolades for the changes that occurred. This principal didn't just walk the talk, he swaggered. It was all "me" and not "we." This was clearly the work of a positivist, instrumentalist leader operating within the modern scientific-objectivist paradigm. After all, isn't a leader supposed to be an expert for others to follow or push aside?

Modern positivism is a philosophy grounded in the objectivity of scientific investigation and one of the major tenets of modern Western civilization. It replaced a dependence on myth and magic and generated the development of our incredible scientific knowledge base. Modern positivism has also generated the thinking that allowed for an understanding of the rules of our capitalistic economic system. The result has been longer, more comfortable lives for millions of people. However, our dependence on this paradigm has value limits.

A core feature of the modern positivist paradigm is the idea that individuals can objectively know and understand the world, including everything and everyone in it (Wheatley, 2006). However, modern thinking is flawed by two assumptions.

The first flaw is the notion that an individual is separate from the elements of her or his environment and can fully understand an observation as a cause-effect relationship. Therefore, anything that occurs can be observed and explained in its entirety. The observer is an objective knower who sees reality. Every event has an identifiable cause, even though antecedents, peripheral elements, and potential consequences that may be connected to the cause-effect relationship are unseen, ignored, or beyond the observer's ability to understand.

The second assumption is that the observer realizes the truth behind the cause-effect relationship. After all, humans are the understanding objective knowers. Therefore, our role is to control events. Objective humans should intervene in cause-effect relationships and thereby judiciously manipulate reality. In the objective world, each individual is the knowing subject and that which she or he sees are objects to be manipulated at will.

A flaw here is that individual subjects will manipulate in ways that interfere with the manipulations of other subjects. These problems are solved by creating organizations that delineate structures containing hierarchical levels of social power. Consequently, some individuals get to be subjects wielding power while others become objects. Problems are observed and defined. Then systems and machines are built to solve them. When a system or machine breaks, it is simply fixed or replaced.

Sometimes hundreds, thousands, or millions of people are used and at times exploited to build machines and systems. Machines extract the materials needed from the earth and systems of machines build other machines. Machines are organized to perform these tasks as efficiently as possible. Everything in the world is viewed as part of a giant machine or a giant system of machines, and this includes people. Now the basic frame for meeting most human needs is the organization, usually pictured as a machine-driven factory (Morgan, 2006; Wheatley, 2006).

The author's work as principal was to be the master machine operator observing and defining problems, then manipulating people and events to fix the obstacles identified. Yes, these manipulations were designed for altruistic purposes and, at the time, those purposes were believed to have been achieved. Although the rightness of the innovations sponsored was never doubted, the strategies and tactics employed in realizing them have become a subject for ongoing examination. The changes were extensions of individual will, and the teachers were the instruments of power. But a school is much more than an extension of a principal's beliefs.

The changes never truly belonged to enough of the people in the school to last. Soon after the author's departure, the changes disappeared as well. Especially doubtful were the leadership practices displayed. Could the political divisions that took place within the school and district have been minimized and success still be achieved? Would different practices have brought along members of the "out-group" or at least more of that group's members to value the changes that occurred? Could a different leadership generate changes that would last?

What could have been done to build lasting change? Perhaps rather than bringing about real change, all the author's stewardship did was continue the status quo system of competition for resources and allegiance—a traditional political power game played very well. Experiences in the author's next principalship helped generate a different view: a more open and inviting leadership that encourages greater participation and collaboration in challenging the status quo.

EVOLUTION STAGE 2: LEARNING TO LISTEN

These personally transforming experiences took place at Aspen Elementary School, a K–6 public school in Los Alamos, New Mexico: the wealthiest, most educated community in the state. Aspen however, serves the poorest section of the district. Although many of the schools' families were affluent and stable, Aspen had the highest student turnover (25 percent) and the highest number of English as Second Language students in the district (11 percent).

The students at Aspen were from more than twenty countries. Some were the children of scientists and technicians from Europe, Asia, and South America who worked at the Los Alamos Scientific Laboratories. Many were children of Mexican immigrants who came to work in low-paying service jobs. The staff and parents were sensitive to a community perception that our school was somehow "less than" the other four elementary schools in the district, but proud to be affiliated with the most diverse school in the community and of the support provided for all students.

At that time, curriculum standards were the fashionable new trend in education circles for the district and the state. Based upon previous success in developing a curriculum-based assessment system, the author came to Aspen as a principal who advocated standards-based education. His belief was that standards would serve as a teacher's tool for assessing each student's learning needs, thereby generating greater individual student success.

The use of standards as an accountability gauge for attempting to assess teacher and school quality or student progression from one grade to another, based entirely on a single standardized measure, had never entered the author's mind. Standards would be a tool to enhance teacher power and responsibility. They would provide a conceptual guide and conversational framework for teachers to use in developing consistent, appropriate, and effective instruction at each grade.

How naïve such thinking was. The teachers' anticipation of future events was much clearer. Standards, once tied to testing, would become a mechanical tool for de-professionalizing teachers and teaching. They became a yoke around the necks of teachers that limited their creativity and their involvement in making decisions about the curriculum and instruction offered to students.

At one of the initial staff meetings, the teachers were divided into groups of four and asked to brainstorm and record their ideas about, "How will our school look, five years from now, when we have developed a standards-based curriculum and instructional system?" The purpose was to generate a list that would put Aspen in line with the district's direction and serve as the basis for the development of a school vision. Listening to teachers as they created their lists in small groups and later to their reports in the reassembled group was a disorienting and unnerving experience for the author.

The teachers didn't regurgitate their support for the district agenda as anticipated. Instead, they vented. In the discussion that followed, the teachers reported their frustration with standards as just another in a long line of reforms. One teacher said that, "Just as soon as we figure out what a reform was about, the district moves on to another reform." They didn't trust the experts previously brought in to present the standards package favored by the central office. Another teacher stated that the presenters had "put down" the district's teachers and teaching. This statement was accompanied by affirmative nods and uh-huh's from most others in the room.

It was clear that the plan for using the teachers' responses as a base for developing a glitzy school vision was not going to work. Each small group of teachers created a list of recommendations for the school and the district. A few of their more salient items were

- We need fewer, broader content standards.
- We must reduce curriculum coverage and concentrate on doing fewer things better.
- We don't need standardized testing. We should develop our own assessments.
- The report card should reflect what the student is doing.

The recorded items were shared by each group and e-mailed to the staff after the meeting. Two of the shared items surfaced deep philosophical issues about standards-based curriculum and instruction. One was that we should focus first on the child, and match the curriculum to the needs of the child. Second, they believed that standards should reflect what skills are really needed for students to become happy, successful, contributing citizens.

This staff meeting was quite discouraging. One reason the author had been hired by the district was to move the standards agenda forward. But the teachers at Aspen were strongly opposed to this. The limits of modern leadership grounded in the objectivity of the positivist framework were surfacing. These teachers were not reacting as intended or anticipated. It seems that manipulating reality is difficult. Actually, as the author eventually learned, it is impossible.

Although shocked by the teachers' responses, the author concluded the meeting saying that, "I'm glad to see that you all are really on board with this standards stuff." They laughed. In retrospect, this meeting was of incredible value for two reasons. The gap between the district administration's view and the views expressed by the teachers had been revealed. More importantly, this meeting represented the beginning of the development of trust between the staff and principal. It was the beginning of the development of safety. It was becoming safe for teachers to express their real, honest opinions.

The author's thinking about the frustrations, concerns, and ideas the faculty shared had been pushed by the revelation of their distaste for the standards framework. Why shouldn't teachers reduce the number of standards so that fewer things could be taught more deeply? Could the school or district create its own assessments rather than depending upon standardized tests? Could the teachers develop a report card that reflected these assessments, and create a plan to support each student who doesn't meet standards?

At the time, the author didn't realize that this meeting set the stage for the work of the school. Rather than setting a vision in line with district expectations, this meeting provided the beginning of a loose, messy, continually evolving mission, defined by and visible through the school culture. This meeting also represented an important step in the author's evolution as a school principal: development toward the practice of a more democratic leadership as a mediator between teachers' perceived needs and district expectations.

Over the remainder of that year, it became common practice to reflect on the teachers' ideas and search for professional literature that supported their assertions. For example, Marzano, Kendall, and Cicchinelli (1998) confirmed the teachers' views regarding the overwhelming volume of content standards. The report said schools would need more than 15,000 hours from kindergarten through grade twelve to cover all of the subject area standards, but schools actually have about 9,000 total hours available for instruction.

As a result of this report, the faculty decided to prioritize district content standards based upon their perception of value for student learning. Content standards were classified as essential, important, and less important or fluff. Third-grade teachers devised the last term. This work eventually extended to all schools in the district and became an important element in the development of a successful new report card.

As a doctoral student, the author had been introduced to and intrigued by the notions of human communication qualities, particularly concerning dialogue and discussion as tools for developing individual capabilities. Of particular interest were two theories. One is *developmental leadership*, a theory developed from the work of Belenky, Clinchy, Goldberger, and Tarule (1986) and Belenky, Bond, and Weinstock (1997).

These researchers analyzed economically poor women's personal growth as they engaged in dialogue sessions. Over time, these disempowered women changed from being "silenced" people who did not understand their ability to know or who thought that others always know more. They developed into "constructed knowers" who recognize that they can and do build knowledge and that others do so as well.

A parallel relationship exists between these disempowered women in their cultural settings and teachers in their work settings. Teaching is a disempowered profession. The work of Belenky et al. led to the creation of the author's conceptual framework labeled *Developmental Empowerment.* This framework identifies teachers' self-views as members of the profession. It contains five teacher development levels; each subsequent level presents a more complex self-understanding of the teaching role and the teacher's responsibility.

Silenced teachers represent the lowest level. These teachers have little confidence in their ability to teach or in students' ability to learn. They are separate from and have little communication with other teachers. They are individuals without a voice, and their primary focus is on individual survival in the classroom and the school. Teaching for them is focused on controlling students.

Teachers who are *received knowers* accepted the status quo. They do not question mandates from above, at least not in public. Some staff members have a basic belief that reforms will fail and therefore accept little responsibility for them and have a predisposition to see new programs in a negative light. Others accept reforms and attempt blanket applications to students. They view their teaching as training.

Subjective knowers generate clarity for understanding curriculum and its impact on students. They accept personal responsibility for neutralizing the negative impacts created by many reform designs. *Subjective knowers* develop a sense of self-efficacy. These teachers begin to focus upon the individual student. Their teaching takes on counseling characteristics. They usually appear to comply with management decisions but behind the classroom door are secretly driven to challenge mandates.

Procedural knowers are reflective and caring individuals who learn and use established procedures to examine students' thoughts and feelings. Procedural knowers are personally reflective. They believe students can learn procedures for solving problems. Teaching in their view is a process of student development. Their classrooms are organized and well managed. They study teaching and attempt to apply practices that others have tested and validated.

Constructed knowing is the highest level of development. Individuals who work as constructive knowers collaborate and co-construct with one another, students, the organization, and the environment. They view the individuals and groups with whom they work as responsible for taking charge in designing and implementing teaching and learning. Artistic and scientific constructivism best describes their philosophical framework and teaching practices. These teachers become true leaders in organizations.

The Developmental Framework provides a way to think about teachers and their work. For example, many of the teachers at the school where the author had previously been principal were *received knowers*. These teachers accepted the status quo and did not think to question it or challenge it. They acquiesced to the whims of authority figures, complied with rules, felt no need to accept responsibility for program failures, and were quick to place blame. They were accountable for doing what they were instructed to do, but not responsible for the outcomes.

Many teachers fit the *subjective* and *procedural knower* classifications. These teachers had a scientific framework for thinking about teaching and accepted programmatic responsibilities. They often blamed themselves for program failures. A number of teachers were classified as *constructed knowers*. For them, teaching was not only a scientific and technical endeavor, but also a very human, individualistic, and artistic calling.

The author believed that engaging teachers in dialogic communications similar to those experienced by Belenky's women would help them move toward the *constructed knower* end of the continuum. The theory was that teachers at every level of the continuum could develop greater understanding of their own knowledge and feel more empowered to have greater influence on their students and one another. Dialogue-based conversations should provide teachers with a greater sense of their own efficacy and enhance their teaching.

Isaacs's (1999a; 1999b) *dialogic leadership*, a framework for working with business leaders, is the second theory that was foundational for this work. When two or more individuals begin to talk together, their talk can extend into a conversation in that the participants share speaking responsibilities in a rotating fashion. As the participants listen and speak, they each make decisions about the relevancy and their level of agreement with what is being said, thereby selecting, processing, and then presenting information.

In other words, conversation participants consider, mull over, or deliberate on what is said in conversation. This generates the need for each participant to choose whether to suspend his or her individual opinions and remain open to hearing what other participants think (dialogue) or to defend the rightness of his or her opposing assumptions (discussion). This is a fundamental choice point in the conversation. The choice to suspend assumptions can lead to open, reflective dialogue that allows for new thinking and ideas to emerge and leads to a shared understanding of the possibilities generated.

If participants choose to defend their views, they make a choice to discuss opinions and assumptions, which generates a second fundamental choice point. Participants may choose to argue a position against another person's position in unproductive defensiveness. As in a political debate, the conversation ends where it begins, with each side maintaining its respective position.

Unfortunately, most conversations in organizations today are focused upon listening to the other participant or participants for flaws in presentation that the listener can use to support her or his case. The focus of the discussion is on winning. Instead, participants may choose to discuss their opinions and assumptions in productive defensiveness. Making such a choice leads to a deep analysis of varying views as participants search for solutions. They become tough on the issues but gentle with each other and are able to focus on learning, assessing, and deciding.

Isaacs recognized the value of leadership based on open communication. He postulated four practices that enable a leader to bring out the best in followers. They are

1. Listening—following deeply another's conversation so that the listener begins to "blend with someone" and to participate fully in understanding how the speaker understands.
2. Respecting—seeing others as legitimate so that one can listen to the sense in what the other is saying.
3. Suspending—our opinions and certainty about our opinions as we display our thoughts (i.e., balancing advocacy and inquiry).
4. Voicing—speaking personal truths to show our genuine selves. (Isaacs, 1999a, p. 4)

STAGE 3 EVOLUTION: LEARNING HUMILITY

The year following the Cerro Grande forest fire, the author began experimenting with open communication systems at Aspen. After experimenting with grade-level sessions for several months, three voluntary, hour-long, open dialogue sessions were sponsored for the faculty. As preparation for the first session the faculty were asked to read Isaacs's "Dialogic Leadership" (1999a) prior to the meeting.

The ground rules for the session were the four dialogic practices outlined above. No formal topics were set for discussion, although the first session was started by sharing a statement made by Linda Darling-Hammond. It was, "The professional teacher in common parlance, is one who does things right rather than one who does the right things" (Darling-Hammond, 1988, p. 61). Teachers were asked what this statement meant to each of them.

Realizing that it is important for a leader to provide ample opportunity for participants to speak, the author limited his statements to requests for clarification or additional information. In most schools, when the principal speaks, all others know that conversation has ended. During the first hour-long session, except to begin and end the meeting, the author spoke only spoke three times, each time asking a question to encourage a speaker to expand on a previous statement.

So that efforts to listen were visual, the author repeatedly moved his eyes from speaker to audience. This was to encourage each participant to speak to the entire group rather than only to the principal. After the first few minutes of the initial session, this was no longer necessary. Teachers soon engaged as if there were no principal present. After recording and transcribing each session, copies were e-mailed to the teachers along with a request for modifications or misinterpretations.

These three meetings sealed the quality of the school culture as open and exploratory. Thereafter, all faculty meetings and interactions had a dialogic quality. The teachers and principal came to a new view of their respective roles. Teachers recognized and accepted the principal's authority for making school-level decisions, but they also recognized their individual and group responsibilities to inform those decisions. That is, the teachers felt both freedom and responsibility to share concerns, fears, objections, and support for the direction the school was taking or could take.

A consensus of understanding developed. This consensus was based upon three elements. First was a belief that all adult school participants were focused upon creating the best learning opportunities for each student. Second was the recognition that each individual had some responsibility for the entire school. Last, participants shared an understanding that it is safe and responsible to express opinions and OK to change opinions in support of, or in opposition to current practice, and to recommend modifications to current practice. That is, teachers and principal can be more than their opinions. Everyone can be a learner.

EVOLUTION STAGE 4: CHALLENGE AS OPPORTUNITY

The experiences in practicing dialogic leadership and analysis of teachers in terms of developmental empowerment led the author to a professional crisis. Most of the teachers at Aspen had great knowledge of their own teaching practices. Their ideas and expertise came to have value equal to or and in some cases greater than the ideas and knowledge of outside experts and district supervisors.

The school, its teachers, students, and community were unique. The author's role was to understand "us" and to understand why policy and program solutions from the district, the state, or hired experts could, at best, provide only partial help for a unique situation. This personal crisis served as the catalyst in the next stage of the author's personal evolution as a school principal. The crisis came to a head after volunteering to lead the district's third-grade teachers in the creation of a standards-based report card.

One of the most treacherous roads a district can travel is attempting to redesign report cards. The previous year, another principal led a committee of first- and second-grade teachers in the creation of a standards-based report card for the primary grades. The product of this committee's work closely resembled the report card developed at that principal's school and became the first report card to be used district-wide.

Teachers across the district disliked that report card and resented the district mandate to use it. Editorial letters in the local paper and testimonials at school board meetings reflected parents' concern that the reporting of students' mastery of standards represented a focus away from providing students with challenging individual instruction and promoting excellence.

The author's priorities (listed in order of importance) were to help third-grade teachers generate a report card that would meet their needs, satisfy parents, and satisfy central office. In order to address the first priority, all of the district's sixteen third-grade teachers were asked to participate in the process of developing the report card. If the teachers developed it, they would find it valuable. Parents, because they valued and trusted their children's teachers, would be satisfied.

At the first meeting, the teachers were surprised that they were not going to take the recently adopted first- and second-grade report card format and apply it to third-grade curriculum. The author explained that we were going to develop a report card that would meet their needs in reporting student progress to parents and that his job as facilitator was to represent their interests to the central office. After three meetings of the full group and numerous sub-group meetings, the group developed a report card that was far different from what the central office and other principals had anticipated.

The draft report card received a very cool reception at a school board meeting. Later, at a closed-door meeting with the district administrative team, the author found himself defending the teacher-generated report card. This was clearly an example of "unproductive defensiveness," a useless but commonly practiced form of debate (Isaacs, 1999b, p. 41). It is merely arguing with one another in order to score points and win the conversation. The problem is that such conversations almost always end leaving participants frustrated and angry. In this case, the district's administrators were angry with the author and he with them.

So, a second meeting was arranged. At this second meeting, the author focused on listening, respecting, and suspending his opinions to truly understand the thinking of these administrators. During the meeting, their objections eventually gave way to questions about why the third-grade teachers developed a report card very different than anticipated. Thus began a dialectic process where, in a series of meetings, the author represented the opinions of teachers to administrators and the opinions of administrators to teachers.

A way to bridge the gap between understanding of the leader's role and the positivist, manager view practiced by administrator colleagues was beginning to surface. The author's role became serving as intermediary between teachers and administrators. This was a new role and one constructed as a result of engaging administrators in open conversation. The author's questions led to others beginning to question their own assumptions. In this role, policy and practice could be challenged and influenced. The power of this role as a catalyst for organizational change was becoming evident.

Listening deeply and carefully to others and truly coming to understand their ideas leads to a speaker's interest in what an inquirer has to say. This is the opening created by dialogue that brings individuals and groups together. Simply put, if someone values what you have to say, then you cannot help but value the other person's opinion. To fully reject the other person's view is to reject your own view. The other's opinion must have value because she or he values your opinion.

Eventually, a report card surfaced that did meet the needs of all groups. All third-grade teachers were informed in an e-mail announcing that the administrative team had unanimously accepted the new third-grade standards-based report card. Almost immediately, most of the district's first- and second-grade teachers sent e-mails asking whether they could revise their report card using the third-grade format.

The following year, the primary teachers revised their report card and all of the district's fourth-grade teachers developed a new fourth-grade report card. Parent surveys after parent-teacher conferences at the end of the first quarter that the new report cards were in place demonstrated much greater acceptance of the new tools for kindergarten and each of the four grades.

CLOSING THOUGHTS: THE LIMITS OF KNOWLEDGE

The stages of the author's evolution as a school leader described in this chapter reveal a transition from a modern positivist leader to a servant leader (Greenleaf, 1977), a constructivist leader (Lambert et al., 1995), and ministerial leader (Sergiovanni, 2008). An essential learning for any inquiry practitioner is recognizing that all individuals construct their own interpretation of reality, whether or not they realize it. However, when groups of people engage in open inquiry grounded in dialogue and discussion, they collectively construct a shared interpretation of reality.

Although individuals in positions of power choose managers, we choose our leaders because they prove themselves as servants, and this service is defined by moral and ethical causes. Inquiry practices transform beliefs. The author was no longer a technically arrogant principal who viewed teachers as instruments to achieve policy outcomes directed by higher authority.

A principal who values the knowledge of teachers develops a strong moral and ethical power. Gitlin and Price (1992) defined "teacher's voice" as "an articulation of one's critical opinion" and a "challenge to domination and oppression" (p. 62). In discovering the teacher's voice, the author found professionalism grounded in relationship and caring, core elements of successful human connections. Many teachers have high levels of knowledge and meaning constructed for their classrooms and their students. They are themselves responsible leaders.

Lambert et al. (1995) identified the development of reciprocal relationships as "the basis through which we make sense of our world" and "continually grow together" or "coevolve" (p. 36). The conversations at Aspen contributed to growing together and provided incentives and a process for challenging the beliefs teachers and principal held individually and collectively and challenged the beliefs of outside experts and administrators as well.

The focus of good teaching is the facilitation of student learning. Good teachers change practice when they perceive that the change is beneficial in their work. Lambert et al. (1995) said, "Constructing school change is a function of 'the conversations'" (p. 82). Therefore, part of the author's leadership focused upon having the conversations that explored possibilities for change with teachers. Another part involved enlisting the support of superordinates in supporting teacher initiatives and mediating on behalf of teachers to reduce the impact of externally developed change policies and directives that often work against the interests of students and teachers.

Smokey's presentation of the policy of preventing forest fires became a personal metaphor for the positivist misinterpretation of human relationships with the natural world and with one another. Rather than protecting nature, our grand attempt at stewardship by preventing forest fires was a damaging interference in the natural cycle of forest renewal. Such knowledge is limited. The author did not know what he thought he knew and neither do those who make such knowledge claims.

This was a most important step in the author's development, and it led to beginning an investigation into the nature of knowledge. Teachers could move along the developmental empowerment continuum in the development of their professional understanding and practice, and the author could do so as well. Individual and collective knowledge evolve. One evening, the author googled "knowledge." The original citation was lost long ago, but it included this quotation:

> Knowledge speaks but wisdom listens.—Jimi Hendrix

And this:

> It is the providence of knowledge to speak and the privilege of wisdom to listen.—Oliver Wendell Holmes

And this:

> These days, people seek knowledge, not wisdom. Knowledge is of the past, wisdom is of the future.—Vernon Cooper

And this:

> Knowledge is proud he knows so much. Wisdom is humble he knows no more.—William Cowper

An investigation into the notion of wisdom was initiated.

Chapter Three

Toward Wisdom

A trip down the aisle dedicated to leadership and management in a bookstore will reveal an abundance of books on these topics. Some of these books look at the leadership qualities of political and historical figures. Many, representative of our society's intense beliefs about free enterprise, have a business focus. These texts often offer step-by-step "how to" guides for becoming an effective and even transformational leader.

So, with the multitude of advice available, why does wise leadership from Wall Street to Pennsylvania Avenue seem so lacking today? Although notions about wisdom and leadership have been closely related throughout history, this relationship has been largely ignored for centuries—an omission that, despite all of the writing on the subject of leadership, may say a good deal about the quality of contemporary thinking.

Our understanding of and interest in the notion of wisdom has clearly been limited by the boundaries of modern positivism. Trowbridge (2005), in a very extensive dissertation, found that there has been very little study of wisdom until the past thirty years. Interest in trying to seek wisdom or understand what is or would be a wise person faded as modernity rejected myth, sorcery, and religion as reflections of truth, replacing it with the development of scientific objectivism centered upon observable, cause-effect relationships.

However, wisdom as a subject of study has recently started to emerge in the management literature. Kessler and Bailey (2007) for example, have organized a *Handbook of Organizational and Managerial Wisdom* that reflects a renewed interest in this subject and contains the work of thirty-seven contributors from psychology, management, and related fields. Kessler and Bailey explained that even though the subject of wisdom has been ignored in the past, it is an important subject. They also recognized that it is a complex subject, because wise people are both rare and more than simply repositories of knowledge.

This chapter addresses the work of some of the authors presented in the Kessler and Bailey (2007) text, as well as other recent work on the subject of wisdom. There are two reasons for this. First, these emerging ideas about wisdom need to be placed in the context of education policy and practice. This is because contemporary education policy, trapped in modern positivism, is a near perfect example of the absence of wisdom. The second reason is that an understanding of these emerging ideas about wisdom substantially contributes to understanding *LTL* practice as a postmodern process for seeking wisdom.

However, before proceeding to a discussion of wisdom, we need to map the philosophical terrain upon which it is placed. Most education theory is grounded in constructivism and social constructivism. Constructivism is a scientifically based understanding of human learning that fits well with pragmatism, the uniquely American philosophical frame. Presented in this text is the pragmatic challenge offered by constructivist theory to education policies that mimic modern mechanical systems. In other words, the thinking behind the policies that mandate standards and testing are quite un-American.

DOORS, WINDOWS, AND MIRRORS

Philosophy is a weighty subject that frightens most people. Therefore, our discussion, although necessary, will be brief. So, let's begin by constructing a little house of understanding: a small and simple metaphorical cabin. After all, the cabin is a national icon and constructing is what Americans do. Such a cabin would contain the beliefs and assumptions of its owner. It contains a door to enter so that the cabin's contents are displayed, a few windows for visualizing some parts of the world outside, and a mirror so that the owner can understand her or his relationships in terms of the world. What might be the contents of such a cabin?

Let's start with the notion of reality. People who believe that there is a real world are referred to as realists. Realism is a philosophical stance grounded in a practical understanding and acceptance of the world. It disavows an idealistic, perfect, or romanticized worldview. Realism assumes that an objective world exists and that our perception(s) allow us to recognize and accept that world. Therefore, a realist would say that we perceive what is.

However, along came the modern period in history. Modernity refers to the period in which industrialization replaced agrarianism as the dominant mode of human activity. The modern period, with its focus on change, challenged realism. It contains the development of capitalism, nationalism, and the ascendency of our belief in the power of science to overcome human ills. For the modernist, change is progress and progress is good. Therefore, what is is changing.

President Dwight Eisenhower once said, "If it is good for General Motors, it's good for America." Of course, he said this long before he suggested that an "industrial military complex" could be very bad for America's people. Back then, it was common for elementary school teachers to present much of their science curriculum in the form of documentary films. The author recalls such films from his own schooling, often sponsored by the DuPont Chemical Company, advocating "better living, through chemistry." Of course, this was before thalidomide babies and the devastating pollution in Love Canal became common knowledge.

So, for the realist, what "is" is, but for the realist of the modern period, what "is" is changing. Modernity, at least in economic terms, has been good for many people, especially for most of the American people. However, for some Americans, such as the members of the thousands of Native American tribes terminated by the economic pursuits of other citizens, it has been very, very bad.

One of the tenets of modernity is objectivism, a focus on scientific cause-effect relationships. The objectivist maintains the realist's view that an external reality exists beyond the mind of the individual. However, modernity also contains the philosophical notion of positivism and human ability to control nature. Indeed, the positivist believes that controlling nature is our job. After all, our superior knowledge requires this. The author's thinking evolution to challenge this notion was explained in chapter 2. Nature did just fine for billions of years without the aid of humans. But under human stewardship, nature seems challenged.

TODAY'S FACTS, TOMORROW'S MYTHS

The modern objective positivist assumes that knowledge can only be acquired or is best acquired through direct observation or experimentation or presented as words from someone with an understanding of it: an expert. A consequence of this belief structure is the assumption that an individual can realize and correctly interpret external reality. That is, if you see it you can believe it. The name we have given each bit of this recognized reality is "fact."

However, the ideas in this text challenge the notions of modern, objective, positivism—or objective, positive, modernity—or positive, modern, objectivity. Please choose the label that works best for you. You have likely made mistakes, so your own personal experiences likely confirm the understanding that a fact is not necessarily true. It is a perception of what is true at any given time. Or, in terms of our cabin metaphor, we see reality through a window of knowing that each of us has constructed; the reflection is filtered by our biological makeup and the culture to which we belong, and then further refracted by individual experiences.

Therefore, a fact may be true, or it may not be true. In fact, a "fact" may in its entirety be an illusion. A fact is something that most people generally assume to be true, real, or actually exist. We just believe a fact is true because either we cannot disprove it, or we have not really tried to disprove it, or perhaps it is just convenient to believe it. Unfortunately, the latter is too often the case.

We know from human history that the facts of one period become the myths of a later time. Here are some examples. Traveling on an ocean was once foolhardy because you might fall off the edge of earth or be eaten by one of the Norse sea monsters mentioned in the preface. In the second century, the Church (there was only one back then) imprisoned Nicolas Copernicus for telling the lie that the earth rotated around the sun. That was long before forward-thinking scientists discovered that the atom was the smallest unit in nature and therefore could not be divided.

In the enlightened American Colonies, it became a fact that witches would put spells on people unless they were burned alive. Until the mid-1800s it was a fact that African Americans were inferior beings. A related fact was that Africans and African Americans needed to be owned by white people because these dark-skinned inferiors were not capable of caring for themselves. Therefore, it was appropriate to buy and sell them. What would those eighteenth- and nineteenth-century knowing and caring stewards think about having an African American president?

At one time, it was a fact that Irish Americans were inferior; then the Italians, the Germans, and of course, Japanese Americans were all spies who were best kept separated from real Americans in encampments. Oh yes, don't forget that the only good Indian was a dead Indian. Of course, this fact began with the fact that Christopher Columbus had landed in India, and not on a new continent. So Native Americans, in fact, became Indians. This just shows that some facts create other facts and both are very wrong.

The mythification of these facts is perhaps more significant than the author's discovery that Smokey the Bear was wrong. But the discovery of the untruthfulness of that fact led to most of the ideas expressed in this text. What facts have you discovered that are not truthful? Today, it is a fact that our children are not learning as much as they have in the past. However, this has been a fact for about four or five generations: a very deep, pernicious fact that grows larger and more threatening every year. The goal of this text is to contribute to the mythification of this fact.

PRAGMATISM: THE AMERICAN CONSTRUCTION

Now two more philosophical frames need to be addressed. One is existentialism, a philosophy based on the assumption that there is no ultimate meaning or purpose in the universe. Therefore, each existentialist is totally responsible for herself or himself. Each creates his or her own world and decides her or his own future. Some of what has thus far been written would seem to support a constructivism grounded in existentialism. After all, a prime theme of the book is the value of individual responsibility.

The constructivist framework that seems to provide a better fit for American education is pragmatism. Pragmatism is a philosophy that grew out of the American experience and serves as a reflection of the best of our nation and provides the grounding we need to address our future. Pragmatism, as the label suggests, is grounded in ideas associated with practicality and seems to come from the idea of *practice*.

So, our knowledge, that is, our truth grows out of our practice, which is a product of our experience. Of course, our experiences are the product of the cause-and-effect observations of which we are aware. This is very similar to modern positivism, except for one element: the job of the pragmatist is to remain doubtful of self-perceptions. We must question our individual perceptions as well as those of others. This is because our perceptions are unique to each individual and they change over time. This idea of change over time is the product of learning.

Perhaps you have a little existentialist buddy running around in your head that makes you want to believe that the meaning you've constructed is factual and true. Doubt is the pragmatist's tool that continually questions those perceptions. Pragmatists must remain doubtful because individual perceptions of the world are inaccurate, incomplete, or just plain false. Recognizing that our perceptions are reflections of reality entering into consciousness through windows of our own construction forces us to continually question the conclusions we draw.

Pragmatists must always try to understand that the truthfulness of the facts or reality being observed is limited by the quality of knowledge represented. However, that little existentialist running around in each of our heads keeps telling us that our windows are perfect in every way. They are clean. They do not bend the light, and we can ignore the mini-blinds that our little buddy installed. By the way, Sigmund Freud named his little buddy "ego."

It seems that realists tend to see answers, existentialists tend to make up answers, and pragmatists are stuck with questions. Consequently, pragmatists continually try to learn. So, this unknowing author is probably not the best person to be a steward of nature. He also has doubts about whether you are capable of adequately providing this stewardship, and as we shall later see, neither are other humans.

So, there is a basic conflict concerning the nature of knowledge between positivism and pragmatism. Pragmatists must avoid assuming that their observations are true representations of reality. They understand that their experiences are limited by the quality of their knowledge and that all knowing is limited by the time in which it exists. So, in spite of Freud's little buddy, it is appropriate to continually clean the cabin's windows, and keep the shades at least partially open. Pragmatists must build on their knowledge by extending and trying to understand personal experiences. They must live questions. They must try to learn.

What is truly wonderful and unique about humans is our ability to share our constructions with one another through communications that enable us to individually construct similar worldly representations. We humans tend to build similar cabins. Right now, the author is sharing his construction of reality with you. This is a door. If these words seem to makes sense, then you have accepted an invitation to come in and see his cabin. Your cabin may be similar, or, if not, you may like this cabin and work to post-modernize your cabin. If so, the author is honored.

This pragmatic view seems to challenge the existentialist notion. If each of us is creating our own world and we are each totally responsible for it, then there is no need to share our ideas. Each of us is in charge of our individual realities. We are responsible only for ourselves and to heck with everyone else. Existentialists don't need any windows or doors, but mirrors would still be nice. They could admire themselves in their perfect cabins.

Nature presents relationships that parallel this representation. Two existentialistic examples are the grizzly bear and mountain lion. They are quite existential creatures who, to the extent they can be, are in charge of their worlds. Nobody tells a grizzly bear or mountain lion what to do. They are in charge, at least until they meet someone with a big gun who can kill them, a large trap that can result in their being imprisoned, or someone of the opposite sex who is really cute. Then, they discover that they may not have very much existential control after all. Additionally, they are both endangered species. So much for existentialism!

EVOLUTION: THE CHANGE PROCESS AT WORK

Now two other windows can more completely reveal the construction of this metaphorical cabin. One is the subject of religion and notions about a higher power. It is approached with some trepidation. After all, those who have questioned religious dogma have often suffered greatly. You have likely heard of the Spanish Inquisition. More recently, we continually read, see, and hear about excesses within fundamentalist Muslim societies.

If you are an existentialist, you probably do not believe in any higher power. How could there be such a presence if you are in charge? But if you do have a religious inclination, then you may be a person who believes that Jesus is the Son of God, or perhaps Mohammad, or Buddha, or all three and that there are other sons as well. So many sons: Oh God, you Devil! Surely God has a sense of humor. Or you may believe there is some energy source, organizer, or something out there that has created an external reality for you to experience: perhaps in happiness, sadness, or both. Maybe this presence is a he, a she, an it, or an all.

Not long ago, the author was driving behind a large, sleek, new automobile driven by an elderly gentleman who, judging by his religious bumper stickers, likely was not an existentialist. One read, "Truth is not relative," so he was likely not a pragmatist either. Pragmatists seem to have difficulty dealing with absolutes. Instead, they look for the relative ability of an idea or supposition to have value for the person who conceives or understands it while recognizing that others may have a differing version of truth and that differing truths may have values relative to situations. This is a reason pragmatists need questions.

So, if you believe there is a presence and recognize your own limitations in understanding that presence, then you are likely a pragmatist, either openly, secretly, or unknowingly. It is also likely that either you believe in a higher power, or don't, or you are like the author and have questions. Although the truthfulness of this previous sentence seems fairly certain, no claim is made that it is factual. Such a statement would be far too authoritative, imposing, and not very pragmatic. Possibility is a window that needs to always remain open.

The final window that needs to be examined on the cabin tour is the concept of evolution. Any discussion of human learning and education would otherwise be incomplete. Darwin's theoretical framework and the modifications that have been made to it since his time provide the best representation available for understanding how we humans have developed and how we may, hopefully, continue to develop in the future. Indeed, we would not be able to conceptualize how humans organize themselves into functioning social units without Darwin's theories or a similar framework.

Darwin explained the development of the great variety of species of organisms through a process of natural selection. This process, he believed, provides the rules through which species have been able to evolve. However, evolution is the change process in perhaps every context. Indeed, Darwin's ideas have been incorporated into systems theory that provides the framework for our understanding of quantum physics, engineering, ecological studies, weather patterns, economies, and much more.

Can you imagine where we would be without the evolution of technology, for example? We would not have computers, or bumper stickers to hang on our sleek new automobiles, or writing, or even words. Without the evolution of organizations we would not have businesses, schools, churches, or families for that matter. In fact, we could not even believe that "truth is not relative" because we could not think it. By the way, the second bumper sticker on that sleek new automobile said, "Evolution is retarded." Hmm!

The point is that the concept of evolution is our description of the operation of the rules of change, as we can understand them. One level, the level that Darwin studied, is biological evolution. The author suspects that his grandmother, several generations back, was an ape named Lucy. He is most grateful to her for his existence. You may reject the notion that you are related to Lucy, and you could be right. Perhaps you prefer not to have the author as a cousin.

However, evolution exists in every aspect of reality that occurs or can possibly occur. Indeed, central ideas of this text are that learning is an evolutionary process. Evolution is change in reality and, until now, Americans have been very good at evolving. How would the driver of that sleek car with the absolute truth bumper sticker explain the evolution of the machine he was driving? It had evolved substantially from the antiquated pickup truck he passed.

Evolution is the driving force in how we humans change our thinking. Remember the discussion of the mythology of fact. Today, scientists see their work in a more postmodern light. Scientific discovery continually turns facts into myths. Evolutionary biologist David Sloan Wilson (2008) for example, sees his work as a way to assure that factual claims are continually questioned and verified.

How about that? Science is evolving; even the science of evolution is evolving. By the way, that old pickup truck had a rear bumper sticker with the words "If you can read this, thank an evolutionarily successful hominid." That sticker was likely referring to Grandma Lucy. But making a judgment based just on those two automobiles would require a concession that God places relatively more value on believers than nonbelievers. Well, maybe not. That would mean God uses a market motive to drive belief. Thank God pragmatists get to have questions!

Fortunately, pragmatists get to fudge on the nature of creation and the operation of the world. They are not in charge of anything other than themselves. Each of us constructs an individual, internal representation of our world and builds windows and doors for sharing these constructions with others, and mirrors so that we may see our own reflections. We are in co-influence relationships, able to look in one another's windows and, when invited, come in through a door, so that we can build a better reality together—or perhaps not.

In modernity, we started building and kept building, but have not spent enough time looking through windows at the objects we have built or in our mirrors to see how those objects are affecting us. We build and assume that what we have built is good and represents progress. This is a big problem in America, but not only America. Modern positivism and the objectivity upon which it depends looks only at what seems to be factual today, assumes this is reality, continues moving in the same direction, and defines this as progress. It doesn't look at the consequences of its own creation. This is why we need to rediscover the ancient notion of wisdom.

WHAT IS WISDOM?

Wisdom has been defined in many ways, but Sternberg's (2004) definition of the balance theory of wisdom is most useful. He said:

> Wisdom is the use of one's intelligence and experience as mediated by values toward the achievement of a common good through a balance among (1) intrapersonal, (2) interpersonal, and (3) extrapersonal interests, over the (1) short, and (2) long terms, to achieve a balance among (1) adaptation to existing environments, (2) shaping of existing environments, and (3) selection of new environments. (Sternberg, 2004, p.164)

The "balance theory" is an appropriate label; this definition attributes wisdom to a balance between individual and group interests and a consideration of that which is near and far away both geographically and in time. Generally, the elements identified in this definition suggest that a wise person has a substantially universal and timeless orientation: a wise person sees broad implications and applications and how both fit with local and more universal contexts to influence future events. So, what processes allow a person to move toward wisdom? How does an individual develop a more timeless and universal orientation?

Bellinger, Castro, and Mills (2004) discuss systems theorist Russell Ackoff's five categories that make up the content of the human mind. Ackoff's categories are data, information, knowledge, understanding, and wisdom. Each category builds upon the previous category in the development of meaning as summarized below.

- Data are simply symbols. Each datum exists and has no meaning beyond its mere existence, such as a date in history.
- Information is data that is organized to be useful and answer questions about who, what, where, and when.

- Knowledge is the application of data and information that answers "how" questions.
- Understanding is an interpolative, probabilistic, cognitive, and analytical process. It is learning rather than memorizing and allows for the invention of new ideas and new knowledge. It allows for seeing possibilities, for synthesis, and thus has a future focus.
- Wisdom is an evaluated understanding. It is extrapolative, non-deterministic, and non-probabilistic.

Wisdom, for Bellinger, Castro, and Mills (2004), is philosophical probing that asks the questions that are difficult to answer. Their view, similar to Sternberg's (2004) view, connects wisdom to values: the framework individuals use to judge between right and wrong, and good or bad. Bellinger et al. (2004) revise Ackoff's hierarchy by placing understanding at the juncture between each of the other four levels. That is, data have meaning when they are organized into information; knowledge is organized systems of information; and wisdom is understanding knowledge in reference to values.

Bellinger et al. (2004) place data as the lowest or simplest category of organization and wisdom at the top as the most complex. However, Lloyd (2006) presented an economics-based framework for thinking about wisdom. He argued that placing wisdom at the top of the reasoning pyramid and data at the bottom reflects the Newtonian mechanistic worldview. Because wisdom is the process for integrating values into knowledge-based decision making, he turned this pyramid upside down. The values of one individual or group, he argued, may be in conflict with the values of another individual or group.

That is, there are different and often competing wisdom frameworks. Therefore, Lloyd suggested that it can be useful to place wisdom at the bottom of the pyramid. An individual or group chooses knowledge, then information, and then chooses data sets based upon the wisdom framework or frameworks from which they began the process. This view certainly provides a way to understand how different individuals and groups can often come to conflicting opinions and decisions and represent multiple perspectives.

One increasingly important change in our postmodern world relates to our growing recognition of complexity. Often the words complex and complicated are used synonymously. However, in systems theory, they have very different meanings. Something is complicated if it has many parts. An automobile engine, as stated at the beginning of the text, is complicated. It has thousands of parts, but each part must relate to every other part in one very specific way for the system to continue to exist. Any change in the relationship between the parts and the engine no longer exists as a system but has become a pile of parts.

However, a family is complex. It might contain only four members: perhaps two parents and two children. Each member has a unique relationship with all others in the family. One of those parents might leave the family due to divorce or death, but unlike the complicated automobile's pile of parts, the family would still exist as a family. Recognition of the notion of systems complexity is becoming increasingly important for understanding the world and for understanding the limitations of modern, objective positivism. This is especially important for understanding human organization, and family is the original example.

The values competition among groups that Lloyd addresses is common today and becoming more common, perhaps exponentially more common—a clear reflection of the complexity of our postmodern world. Human relationships have always been complex, but in the past this was not recognized, nor was it so important to recognize it. Human communities were more localized and members of those communities were more alike. However, today, we talk about a global community, so that conflicting wisdom frameworks and knowledge sets can be accessed from anywhere in the world in an instant.

Years ago as a new elementary school principal serving a rural, predominately Catholic area, the author expected to discover general acceptance of a shared set of values within the community. One day, he sent home an announcement asking parents not to send their children to school for Halloween parties with "scary witches' masks." The following morning, it was necessary to apologize to a delegation from the Wiccan community. Even that small rural isolated community was becoming more complex.

Today a decision maker or group working to make a decision must come to understand the nature of value conflicts and come to choose between or integrate those conflicts before making a decision. Essentially, both individual decision makers and groups working toward a decision must negotiate competing wisdom frameworks. The qualities, that is, the wisdom, of such decisions can be measured by the level of timeless and universal acceptability achieved.

However, this process begins by understanding, appreciating, and valuing the qualities in conflict among competing wisdom frameworks. Stated another way, it begins by discovering and pragmatically accepting the relative conflicting values of a diverse community and seeking to construct a level of understanding and consensus within the community that incorporates the best of those characteristics.

Stated one more way, moving toward wisdom is a product of the *LTL* process. Therefore, *inquiry* through dialogue and discussion are at the core of successful decision-making processes. Today, an individual decision maker or a group hoping to come to a decision must develop an understanding of values/wisdom-based conflicts, and then choose what knowledge sets from those wisdom traditions should be considered, and what information is required to develop further questions.

According to Lloyd (2006), "it is our values/Wisdom that defines the limits of what we consider acceptable in the first place, and that decision then determines our knowledge/action priorities, which then determines what information is required and that determines what further questions need to be asked about the data required" (p. 5). Consequently, inquiry by a leader or inquiry by the members of a group can lead to greater understanding of both values-based conflict and possibilities for solutions to those conflicts. We will return to this topic in chapter 7.

KNOWLEDGE LIMITS AND THE NEED FOR WISDOM

Chapter 2 presented the reflective thinking and experiences that led to construction of the author's post-positivist philosophical framework and development of *inquiry* practices with teachers and administrators. The positivist/objectivist philosophical stance reflected through quantitative analysis is bounded by the limits of scientific objective "knowledge." Modern knowing is limited by the interpretation of limited facts as complete truths. Inquiry provides avenues for individually and collectively challenging and testing these assumptions, so that we can learn to recognize the limits of what we know.

Positivists view the world and everything in it as known or knowable. The positivist looks at objects as elements to be manipulated. Unfortunately, the modern positivist's view has traditionally been limited by the assumption of superior knowing. That is, reality for the positivist consists only of that which is known and discoverable. She or he can see the many complicated parts, but not the complex and hidden relationships between and among the parts.

This view of reality operates within a set of accepted assumptions. These assumptions are at best hypotheses tested in narrow isolated arenas revealing relationships that are visible, knowable, and perhaps complicated. However, this perception of reality misses asking the questions that suggest the possibility of an unknown complexity. How different is the modern positivist from the beneficiary of received "truth"? How different from the elderly driver of the sleek new automobile who used bumper stickers to display his certainty that "Truth is not relative" and that "Evolution is retarded."

The modern positivist's objectively discovered "truth" represents a view that is likely more truthful than the mythology it displaced. However, the human history of continually replacing facts suggests that "the truth" is not *the* truth. Perhaps the modern positivist is actually caught in an existential trap assuming her or his experimentally acquired representation of "facts" and "truth" is reality? Maybe the modern positivist tricks himself or herself into thinking that the elements of fact they are able to witness are total reality. Modern positivists do not know what they think they know because truth evolves.

Are we reaching the limits of our dependence upon positivistic, scientific objectivism in the same way that centuries before we recognized the limits of myth, sorcery, and magic? Do we need to surface pragmatic doubt? Are there undiscovered, hidden relationships that have important implications beyond what we know or can know in the present? Should we search for hidden complexities to shake up our positivist certainty? Robert Oppenheimer's statement posted in chapter 2 about his realization of the limitations of the objective view and the technical arrogance it sponsors reflected his discovery of the limits of positivist thinking.

The technical arrogance of the modern objective positivist described by Oppenheimer and the instrumentalism to which it leads points to a deep flaw in our national character that has repeatedly led to oppression, subjugation, economic calamity, and ecological disaster. Perhaps the most significant example is our history of slavery and its justification as necessary for the protection of the enslaved. The removal of native peoples from traditional homelands, their placement on reservations, and the removal of children from their families and placement in boarding schools so they could learn to be successful "like whites" is another example.

False assumptions of positive knowing have been a dominant theme in American history. The poor and laboring classes, including children, were continually abused during the second half of the nineteenth century and first half of the twentieth century. But the idea of superior knowing and associated technical arrogance extends beyond the disadvantaging and mistreatment of minorities and the laborers of the past.

Historian Patricia Nelson Limerick (1987) extended the idea of this arrogance to the conquest of the environment in the western United States. Her thesis connected with the author's experience of the Cerro Grande forest fire in New Mexico described in chapter 2 and with ongoing environmental, economic, and social issues that afflict us today. She presented the story of Gifford Pinchot's visit to the Grand Canyon with naturalist John Muir in 1897.

One evening at camp, Pinchot and Muir "encountered a tarantula. Pinchot wanted to kill it, but Muir defended the spider, arguing that it had a right to be there" (Limerick, 1987, pp. 293–94). Pinchot, who within ten years would become the developer and inspirational leader of the U.S. Forest Service, believed that his responsibility was to tame the Wild West. His job was "not to stop the axe, but to regulate its use" (p. 298).

The dominant view in Pinchot's time was that the American frontier is the line of westward movement. After settlement, the land is civilized and saved. The previously untamed lands gain value as farm, mine, and energy producer. The land and what lies under it are objects for use by a knowing human, the positivist, who gives value to the land. Pinchot's natural world was improved by human intervention.

Limerick argued that the idea of taming the frontier is still alive. "Frontiers," she said, "involve mules, horses and oxen but not jeeps; pickaxes and pans but not air drills and draglines; provisions in sacks and tins but not freeze dried packets; horse drawn plows but not mechanized combines with air-conditioned drivers' modules; bows and arrows but certainly not nuclear tests in Nevada; amateurs but not engineers" (Limerick, 1987, p. 24).

She concluded that

> Many American people have long held to a faith that humans can master the world—of nature and humans around them, and Western America put that faith to one of its most revealing tests. A belief in progress has been a driving force in the modern world; as a depository of enormous hopes for progress, the American West may well be the best place in which to observe the complex and contradictory outcome of that faith. (Limerick, 1987, pp. 29–30)

The frontier thinking that Limerick described is still dominant. In the Cerro Grande fire, we lost hundreds of homes because for many years we had believed that preventing forest fires was fulfilling our role as stewards of the land. We truly believed that preventing fires supports forests. Unfortunately, there is substantial evidence that we are failing to learn that we don't know what we think we know.

Thirty years ago the tanker *Exxon Valdez* was draining its contents onto the Alaska Coastline. While this paragraph was written, the southern coast of the United States was quickly being covered in oil spilled from British Petroleum's blown-up Deep Water Horizon oil rig. Should we extend the frontier designation to the Gulf of Mexico? What about the severe economic downturn beginning in 2007–2008 that has come to be called "the Great Recession"? Unfortunately, by the time you read this, there will likely be several more events in which human technical arrogance has played a substantial role.

Maybe we should include bankers, mortgage industry leaders, and auto manufacturers as frontier thinkers. What about the political thinking that led us into the war in Afghanistan, the longest war in our history. The League of Nations was founded over ninety years ago. Its purpose was to make the world safe for democracy. It didn't. Truthfully, our knowledge is limited: we humans, at any given time, do not know what we think we know.

Chapter Four

Limiting Knowledge Limits Future

The previous chapter addressed our growing understanding of the limitations of knowledge and the consequent technical arrogance occurring as a product of dependence on and trust in a modern, objective, positivist paradigm. Perhaps the most important implication of these limitations of human knowledge and our failure to understand them relates to the choices made in preparing our children for the future.

The absolute but mistaken faith in knowledge of the modern positivists is as visible in our schools today as it was previously for the justification for slavery, the relocation of Native Americans, and the "taming" of the frontier. Current school policies and procedures continue to reflect "frontier thinking." Ideas such as *No Child Left Behind* (2001) and *Race to the Top* (2010) are no more refined than Smokey the Bear's continuous admonition that "Only you can prevent forest fires."

Contemporary education policies cause complex outcomes that contradict their intent. These policies interfere with the development of the creative and innovative thinking that our young must develop. They fail to provide our young with the creative opportunities required for the development of the new knowledge that our nation requires in order to maintain our status in the world. These policies violate the intent of the founders of this nation and our beliefs about fairness, justice, equality, and democracy. Additionally, these polices limit our international role as a model for democracy and justice.

The ideas contained in these policies are nearly perfect representations of the knowledge limits generated by the "frontier thinking" of modern positivists. These limits are becoming increasingly visible in our complex world. This chapter begins the analysis of the thinking that has led to the misinterpretation of reality represented by these policies. These strategies clearly lack the universal and timeless orientation that wisdom-seeking policies would provide. Consequently, they point to the urgency of our need for developing *LTL* practices.

STANDARDS ARE LIMITS OF POSSIBILITY

The purpose of curriculum standards is to provide a framework that will produce a high-quality education for all children. The effect of these requirements has been standardization. The range and variety of curriculum choices and learning opportunities available for students are becoming more limited or altogether eliminated. Consequently, each student in the classroom or grade in the school receives very similar instruction, delivered at about the same pace. The assumption here is that quality education for all is closely related to the same education for all, regardless of each student's prior knowledge, talent, interests, and abilities in each area.

Additionally, our positivist-framed education policies are increasingly focused on assessing, through standardized tests, the increasingly limited set of curriculum elements. Teachers are accountable for enabling each student to annually deliver mostly correct answers to twenty-five to seventy secretly maintained test items in core curricular areas. These core areas generally include reading, math, and science, but not much else. Is the primary goal of education in America to reduce difference and generate similarity among its younger population? Is this what we really want for our children? Do we want to define equal opportunity as sameness?

One of the most important discoveries in systems science has significant implications for understanding the increasing complexity of human social systems. It is the law of requisite variety developed by John Ross Ashby in 1958 (Heylighen and Joslyn, 2001). The variety of responses available to any system must be equal to or greater than any demand or set of demands made by the environment. If the system does not have an option or set of options to respond to a change in environmental demand, then that system will fail.

As an illustration of requisite variety, let's examine one of the great products of modernity: the automobile, a nearly perfect expression of the modern period and modern America in particular. It is also a wonderful example of a complicated machine and an ideal example for a discussion of systems. A subsystem of the car is its windshield wipers. They operate at a limited variety of speeds.

Imagine that you are driving along the interstate during a heavy rain and a large tractor-trailer rig passes by, throwing up a wall of water that blocks your vision. You turn your wipers to high speed continuous, but still cannot see. Applying Ashby's law of requisite variety provides an explanation for what happened. The windshield wipers subsystem of the automobile was inadequate to meet the needs demanded by a change in the environment: the sudden high water volume flowing onto the windshield from the tractor and trailer wheels.

In the introduction of this text, the automobile was presented as a very complicated system. It is complicated because all of the parts work together in only one way. But how does Ashby's law apply to a complex system in which the elements of the system fit together in many different ways? Are there complex human systems relevant to an application of requisite variety? Let's see how this notion applies to schools.

Armstrong (2006) presented a very strong case against the limitations of current education policies framed around curriculum standards. He defined "academic achievement discourse" as "the totality of speech acts and written communications that view the purpose of education, primarily as supporting, encouraging, and facilitating a student's ability to get high test grades and standardized test scores in school courses, especially in courses that are part of the core curriculum" (p. 10).

According to Armstrong, "academic achievement discourse" has created a crisis in American schools. He said that the most recent "cause of this crisis is the No Child Left Behind Act of 2001" (Armstrong, 2006, p. 7). Academic achievement discourse, he argued, relegates schools to delivery of a required uniform curriculum for all students, limits learning to the purpose of securing a high-paying job, and justifies the imposition of top-down policy mandates. These top-down mandates are products of the previously described frontier thinking based on the technical arrogance of policy makers.

Much of the education discussion over the past thirty or so years has clearly had an academic achievement discourse focus. This has had enormous implications for students, teachers, and schools. Academic achievement discourse is clearly a product of the modern positivist framework. It has resulted in increasingly complicated policies made up of more and more parts in the form of rules and regulations. But it has ignored the complexities of the nature of learning and human motivation. It continues to represent children as empty vessels into which all we need to do is pour knowledge; it ignores the changing qualities of each generation of students.

MOTIVATION, MARKETS, AND IRRATIONAL HUMANS

International venture capitalist Robert Compton recently spoke at a conference on mathematics and science education sponsored by the author's university. Mr. Compton discussed how much harder his non-American employees worked and how motivated they were by money. In contrast, he told a story about a brilliant young American college graduate who had previously worked for him. This former employee was not particularly motivated to maximize his earnings potential. When asked why he wasn't working to earn as much money as he could, the brilliant young man simply said that he was "not coin operated."

Mr. Compton used this statement to support notions about the risks our nation faces because, he argued, our young are not adequately motivated by money. Perhaps Mr. Compton missed the central point of his own story. It is likely true that this young man and many other young Americans are not particularly motivated by money. At least they are not motivated only by the need to acquire money. Yet, the academic achievement discourse education program that Mr. Compton was advocating is designed around the idea that they are so motivated.

Mr. Compton's view is straightforward modern, cause-effect, technically arrogant, limited frontier thinking. Frankly, it is encouraging that our young people are not totally "coin-operated." Their motivation is more complex than that. Economists and psychologists have long known, and business people are now discovering, what this young employee of Mr. Compton's seemed to tacitly understand. External motivators like money have important limitations, and much of the work done in America today and likely to be done in the future is more dependent on internal motivation.

Abraham Maslov developed a theory that has been generally accepted because it provides such a practical description of why we humans behave as we do (Simons, Irwin, and Drinnien, 1987). He was a humanistic psychologist who believed that humans are not controlled by mechanistic forces. Instead, we strive to become self-actualized by developing our individual potential. Humans want and need to be creative. He believed that people start with a weak disposition and move toward self-actualization to the extent that their environment provides support for doing so.

Maslow identified a hierarchy of five levels of basic needs, from lowest to highest, as follows.

- Physiological or biological needs include requirements for air, water, food, and warmth.
- Safety needs are the need to feel secure and generally are not apparent except during emergencies. However, most of us have seen the image of a small child hiding behind a parent: clearly an expression of the perception of not feeling safe.
- Need to be loved and to belong.
- Need for esteem and the respect of others.
- Need for self-actualization. The individual pursues the area or areas of endeavor that are rewarding for that individual.

The ability of each individual to move along this hierarchy depends upon the support provided by the environment. An individual feels discomfort at whatever level her or his needs fail to be met. As the needs are met at each level, an individual's next higher level will surface. It is rather easy to experiment with the lower-level needs. Try holding your breath for as long as you can. In a few seconds you will likely begin to feel rather restless and uncomfortable. Perhaps next you would like to try walking across a big city freeway during rush hour. OK, don't. You get the idea. It looks as though you can recognize yourself in Maslov's hierarchy.

However, at each higher level of needs more time is usually required for discomfort and restlessness to set in. Many of us can actually be alone for several days before feeling lonely. Perhaps at the higher levels we get to do a little banking. It seems that a little love can go a long way. Indeed, some solitude actually helps with many kinds of work. Solitude allows a deeper, keener focus that can contribute to becoming more self-actualized.

Dr. Maslov expressed his belief that, for many people, much of the environment does a poor job in helping the individual move up the hierarchy. Think of the millions of people in some of the African nations who are starving or the people of Haiti who live in tent cities after the devastating earthquake that stuck that island. Closer to home, think of the people of New Orleans and the Gulf Coast, who suffered through Hurricane Katrina, and several years later have still not recovered. Maybe closer to your home, think of the more than 20 percent of American children who live in a state of poverty. Some of them are likely in your community.

Most people in America who are not living in poverty have their psychological/biological and safety needs met. So, they must be focused on higher-level needs. Now think of Mr. Compton's former employee, who was not "coin-operated." This young man sounds like an intelligent, well-adjusted young American whose lower-level needs are being met and who is more interested in becoming self-actualized than he is in earning more money. This young man's lack of interest in earning more money likely means that he feels he has enough coinage and is ready to apply his energy to more meaningful, socially rewarding tasks.

Daniel Pink (2009) has written a text entitled *Drive*. It updates Dr. Maslov's hierarchy and gets to the heart of the gap between our contemporary knowledge of human motivation and most organizational motivation practices. He identifies three levels of motivation that he called 1.0, 2.0, and 3.0. He describes motivation 1.0 as the basic biological drive associated with physiological needs such as hunger and thirst. Motivation 2.0 is the external motivation perhaps first written about as it relates to organizations by Frederick Winslow Taylor in the early 1900s and advocated today by individuals like Mr. Compton and other modern frontier thinkers.

Taylor's scientific management is the embodiment of the modern positivist mentality and a celebration of the machine as the appropriate metaphor for organizations. Pink argued that the bedrock assumption of this framework is that the key to success in any organizational endeavor is to reward the good and punish the bad. Taylor's assumption was that people must be managed with carrots and sticks, or in Mr. Compton's case "coins." When someone produces more of what the manager wants, then that person is rewarded with more money, a better office, or some other material reward. This is an accurate explanation of motivation for many types of work.

Carrots and sticks work well for algorithmic tasks like the production of goods in factories. These tasks require developing a solution for a specific problem, such as moving goods from point A to point B, or assembling parts into a finished product as efficiently as possible. These tasks can be complicated. But carrots and sticks don't work well for heuristic tasks that require creativity and complex problem solving that may involve several solutions or multiple levels of solution. In fact, the overuse of such material rewards often interferes with the motivation needed for such tasks.

What makes creative and complex tasks different is that rather than working to receive a reward for task completion, the performances of such tasks are themselves rewarding. This has certainly been true for the author in writing this text. The challenge of making sense of diverse ideas has presented many "aha" moments, and arranging them in an organized fashion provided a sense of accomplishment.

Anyone who has a hobby experiences what Maslov theorized, Pink described, and the behavioral psychologists have found. Golfers are good examples. Except for a very small number of professionals, players receive no monetary reward. Additionally, for many of us who attempt the game there frequently seems to be no reward of any kind. Even after a very bad day on the links, a dedicated golfer cannot wait until the next opportunity to play, just hoping to discover the magic that will make for a better score. The challenge of the task was the reward.

The lack of coin motivation in Mr. Compton's former employee is actually quite typical. Coins are motivating to people who need a sufficient income to meet their physiological, biological, and safety needs. Coins also work for some workers as substitutes for love and the respect of others. We can apply this motivation to bankers, Wall Street financiers, and perhaps Mr. Compton. But coins are not good motivators for most individuals who feel comfortable and secure. Such individuals are motivated by the challenges of complex tasks and often by a sense of service to and for others. Sufficiently paid educators usually fit in this category.

Providing extrinsic motivation for tasks that are intrinsically rewarding can actually interfere with the performance of those tasks. What we have experienced in the United States is that we have outsourced more and more of that routine algorithmic "coin" motivated work to other countries or replaced it with improved technologies. How likely is it that most of those lost factory jobs are going to return to America? It's not very likely at all. So choosing to be coin-operated is not a very useful option for most of our young people.

Many of our young need to and want to work toward self-actualization in a motivation 3.0 type of environment. This is the reason that schools are so important. Education can provide our young with the higher-order thinking and learning skills that, when paired with motivation 3.0, can enable them to create the organizations and products our future requires. But current education policies focused on curriculum standards and testing are largely dedicated to developing the algorithmic skills required for "coin operation." Success for our newer generations requires developing the heuristic higher-order thinking and learning skills the future demands.

However, let's assume for a moment that those who advocate the academic achievement framework are correct. Americans are or should be motivated by carrots and sticks. A kindergarten teacher would need to be an expert in kindergarten curriculum. However, that teacher wouldn't need to know much about child psychology, how the brain learns, or understand the needs of diverse children or the needs of children of poverty. The teacher would not need to know why Lacresha is so quiet, why Tommy is bullying other students, or why Carmen seems to have trouble remembering what she learned from one day to the next.

Motivating students would be simple. She or he could just bribe them using candy or "coins" to learn a predetermined number of letters and sounds each month. Then test them at the end of each month. We could even apply some multiplier for the total number of letters, sounds, and words a class learns in a month and use this as payment for the teacher. Think about it: education as piecework. It would all be so simple and straightforward. By George, we would finally be getting a decent return on our education investment.

Unfortunately, recent school and teacher accountability reform models are not much more sophisticated than this. The positivist argument is that the job is simply to transmit the grade level curriculum to each student. We would have no need for teachers who would stretch their students beyond "coin" operation motivation systems. We would not need teachers who understand and build upon complex, intrinsic motivation. We would not be concerned about unfolding the unique development of each student and inspire her or him to reach beyond grade-level competencies and develop his or her individual talents and creativity.

Coin-operated students may exist in other countries. However, are they the students our society needs or wants? If we remain in an academic achievement discourse mindset, from where will the creative adults come who will challenge us to discover that we do not know what we think we know? Who will invent our future? It will likely not be Americans.

Dan Ariely is a behavioral economist and psychologist at Duke University. He studies and experiments with judgment and decision making or JDM as he labels it (Ariely, 2009). His background in economics and psychology has allowed him to develop a unique understanding of our behavior. He has concluded that the economic model based upon assumptions of rationality and typically used to define human behavior just doesn't work. He says that we humans are in fact, *"predictably irrational* [and] that our irrationality happens the same way again and again" (Ariely, 2009, p. xx; author's italics).

The reason Ariely has identified for our irrationality comes from the conflict between the social norms and the market norms that make up the rules of our lives. Social norms are "wrapped up in our social nature and our need for community" (p. 76). Social norms are operating when you open a door for a person carrying a large object, help your neighbor move a couch, or prepare dinner for a sick friend. Market norms are based on sharp-edged exchanges based upon costs and benefits, such as wages and prices. Our problem is that often market and social norms get mixed in the real world and as a result we behave irrationally.

A central difference between social norms and market norms is the idea of reciprocity. If market norms prevail, we expect immediate reciprocity. That is, something is sold and something is bought. However, if social norms prevail we either postpone reciprocity or don't expect it at all. We take part in the exchange because we are social beings and care about one another.

One of many examples Ariely (2009) provides relates to appropriate behavior at a dinner given by a mother-in-law. If market norms prevailed in such a situation, it would be appropriate to pay the mother-in-law for dinner. But because social norms prevail in this situation, such a payment would likely create a major family crisis. Chances are the payor would not be re-invited to dinner by the payee for a long time. It seems that mothers-in-law, like Mr. Compton's young friend, are not "coin-operated" and yes, they are complex as well.

The problem is that when we mix norms we become irrational. But Ariely (2009) suggests that our irrationality is predictable. One area he has examined is the use of bonuses and gifts by employers to improve job performance. Money and other tangible incentives, he has discovered, are very often the most expensive way to motivate people. Social norms are not only cheaper, but often more effective.

Ariely sees important implications for our schools from his findings. He said that "standardized testing and performance-based salaries are likely to push education from social norms to market norms" and that "more testing is unlikely to improve the quality of education" (Ariely, 2009, p. 93). Indeed, the author prefers that his grandson's second-grade teacher be motivated by social norms rather than market norms. She should love and care for the child as a person with an unlimited learning potential that can be developed, rather than a knowledge constricting test score that might earn her a bonus.

Ariely (2009) suggested that more likely approaches to improving schools lie in rethinking curricula and "linking them in more obvious ways to social goals (elimination of poverty, and crime, elevation of human rights, etc.), technological goals (boosting energy conservation, space exploration, nanotechnology, etc.) and medical goals (cures for cancer, diabetes, obesity, etc.) that we care about as a society" (p. 93). He believes that such a linkage would likely contribute to parents, teachers, and students seeing and valuing a larger social goal frame and as a result become more motivated.

Mr. Compton's young friend and many, perhaps most young Americans are seeking this kind of motivation. Such goals are for most people clearly more inspiring than "coin-operated" motivation. Pursuing such goals requires individuals who are internally motivated, or as Dr. Maslov would say, pursuing self-actualization in a system that Dan Pink would describe as operating at motivation 3.0.

POLITICALLY PRODUCED CRISIS: SCHOOL FAILURE

The Manufactured Crisis: Myths, Fraud, and the Attack on America's Public Schools is the title of a book written by David Berliner and Bruce Biddle (1995). Even though written almost two decades ago, it has served as a prologue for what was to come in the education policy world. The title is still a perfect representation of the dangers of the positivist thinking practiced by politicians. This perception of crisis in education will be discussed in the next several pages. It truly is a myth, and it has perpetuated a fraud. Now this lie is reaching very dangerous proportions.

However, the argument presented here is not that politicians intended to perpetuate a fraud upon the American people, although many have said exactly that. Instead, trapped by the limits of modern positivist thinking, they or at least the vast majority of them have believed that the manufactured crisis was real. They believed that they could use this crisis to their advantage and at the same time contribute to improving the quality of schooling. However, the results of their success in selling the manufactured crisis have been very damaging for schools and the nation.

Gerald Bracey (2004) challenged these misconceptions about education in the United States throughout much of his life. He concluded that these misrepresentations are a tactic designed to "make people fear for the future," so that "you can control them" (p. 210). The need to control is a function of the management paradigm that began with Frederick Taylor's notion of scientific management in the early 1900s, but has been well adapted by politicians.

The fraud Berliner and Biddle discovered in 1995 still dominates education policy thinking. Whether perpetuated intentionally or unintentionally, it damages schools, the people who work and learn in schools, and the relationships between the schools and the communities they serve. Unfortunately, politicians are very good salespeople. This damage is worsening over time, as the politicians have become better at regenerating the crisis and creating policies that extend their market-framed controls more deeply into the work of schools and teachers.

The thinking limits of politicians could ultimately lead to the final demise of public schooling and to the demise of America as the inspirational and ethical leader of our planet. The next several sections address some of the elements of the "manufactured crisis" that led to Berliner and Biddle's conclusion and extend their arguments to policies and events that have occurred in the seventeen years since the publication of their text.

REAL CRISIS: STANDARDIZING THE FUTURE

An important, recently published text is Yong Zhao's (2009) *Catching Up or Leading the Way*. Dr. Zhao was educated as a child and young adult in China. Therefore, he knows Chinese education practices at both a professional and personal level. He has presented a strong argument against our current focus on curriculum standards and student assessment through standardized testing. He wrote about the development of the world's first standardized test: a Chinese civil service test developed in the sixth century AD.

Zhao explained that until the advent of that civil services test, China was the world leader in innovation, inventing such things as movable type, gunpowder, and the magnetic compass. But this test, developed and used to identify all of the emperor's high level servants, marked the beginning of the decline of China's ascendency. For centuries an individual's score on this test was the primary way to move up the social and economic ladder.

Individuals in China would spend their lives preparing for, taking, and retaking this test because placement in the emperor's social order did not depend upon individual accomplishments. Placement depended on test performance. It was the world's first high-stakes test, and its effect was to limit the variety of skills and talent available to address the needs of the empire. In other words, this test effectively reduced the requisite variety Imperial China needed to adapt to changing environments.

Zhao (2009) concluded that most Americans now believe that education is in crisis due to two achievement gaps. One is an international gap in which we are losing an education race to countries like China and India. Those who support this argument use international standardized test comparisons. These arguments are speculative at best. For example, Zhao reported Keith Baker's study of the relationship between countries' performances and indicators of well-being. Baker found either no correlation or a negative correlation between the two. This manufactured fear will be addressed in greater depth in chapter 5.

The other education gap is a domestic one that compares inner city poor and minority student test scores and graduation rates with their suburban peers. This is a very real, long-standing, and ongoing crisis. Zhao (2009) faults blaming this crisis on "teachers and school leaders who [the critics believe] are unwilling or unable to hold high expectations of their students and deliver high quality instruction because they have become complacent or lazy" (p. ix). A more truthful examination reveals that the greatest barrier to student learning is poverty. How has this barrier been addressed?

Jonathon Kozol has studied, written about, and criticized the role of poverty, segregation, and more recently the re-segregation of schools in America. He argues that we seem to have accepted a dual education system in which the nation's poor, mostly minority young people, attend poorly funded, poorly functioning schools where "the sweetness of too many of these inner city children [becomes] corroded. Some of it may be replaced by hardness, some by caution, some by calculation rooted in unspoken fear" (Kozol, 2005, p. 10). These children have learned to distrust almost everything in their lives, including adults and schools.

Zhao argued that standards and testing are resulting in public acceptance of test scores as the only measure of performance for students, teachers, and schools. The problem is that this focus leads to classroom instruction that centers more and more on only tested areas. Zhao's fear is that standards and their assessment through testing will produce "a homogeneous group of individuals with the same abilities, skills, and knowledge" (p. x).

Do we want to follow the Chinese model? Will making our children more alike contribute to developing the creativity they need? Will academic achievement discourse provide the requisite variety the American system needs? Will testing and focusing instruction on narrow, tested standards enable the children of our poorest citizens to move up the social and economic ladder? Such practices contribute to the vicious cycle of mistrust and failure that Kozol (2005) described and decrease the motivation to learn.

Paul Houston, former executive director of the American School Administrators Association, said that the authoritarian, test-based reform model we currently have is destined to fail (Houston, 2007). This was a brave statement during the reign of *No Child Left Behind*. Houston discussed an article from

Newsweek International in which editor Fareed Zakaria reported on a very revealing interview with the education minister of Singapore.

Singapore at that time had the highest tests scores in global rankings and those scores were often used to demonstrate the weakness of science and math education in the United States. Zakaria asked why American students who tested much worse, do much better ten to twenty years later, especially as inventors and entrepreneurs. The minister said that both the United States and Singapore are countries based on meritocracies: America's is based on talent and Singapore's is based on test scores.

Will academic achievement discourse and standardized test-based assessments develop the skills and talents we need to continue leading the world in innovation and entrepreneurialism? Will the modern positivist framework develop the adaptive individuals the future will require? Or will the United States become the Imperial China of the postmodern world? Will we be trapped in a continuous cycle of decline? If most of our nation's schools serving large numbers of impoverished and minority students are any indication, we are well on our way to closing that trap.

Armstrong's, Zhao's, Kozol's, and Houston's ideas are not new. Susan Ohanian (1999) argued against the idea of standards and standardization. She clearly presented the limits of the positivist-objectivist framework. She said that "people designing curriculum standards have the notion that knowledge is pure and unrelated to the knowledge seeker" (p. 9). She called these people "Standardistos" and said

> Whether Standardistos are hawking NAFTA [North American Free Trade Agreement], which ended up decimating U.S. jobs, or a uniform curriculum, which will end up causing the dropout rate to skyrocket, the language is the same. Standardistos talk in universe-speak, using such cosmic terms as *all workers, global economy, world-class skills, world-class children.* But when they get the phonemes and the math facts all lined up in neat and tidy rows, what Standardistos really offer is a classroom universe of narrow isolation. (p.13)

Ohanian (1999) echoed Parker Palmer's idea about the personal nature of teaching. She said, "We teachers, particularly those of us in elementary schools, teach who we are. We are the curriculum" (p. 9). In contrast, she quoted Bob Dulli, vice president for geography education at the National Geographic Society, as he congratulated the California Academic Standards Commission on their efforts to be on "the cutting edge" of performance standards.

Mr. Dulli recommended that "the more specific and concrete the standards are, the better the possibilities are for teachers and parents to understand what students must learn" (p. 74). This statement clearly represents the positivist-objectivist view. Dulli's statement revealed his belief that the commissioners own the knowledge: they are the knowing stewards of what children's future will require.

Positivists like Mr. Dulli, who have acquired positions of authority and power, believe they have superior knowledge. Their positivist worldview defines a narrow reality that is limited by their individual experiences. They know, because they define what "knowing" is. Consequently, they believe they are better able to make decisions about the needs of students than are the teachers and parents who know those students. Unfortunately, little has changed in the decade since Mr. Dulli presented his view.

We are in the process of developing national "common core standards" pushed by the National Governors Association (Core Standards.org.). The purpose statement of the core standards follows.

> The Common Core State Standards provide a consistent, clear understanding of what students are expected to learn, so teachers and parents know what they need to do to help them. The standards are designed to be robust and relevant to the real world, reflecting the knowledge and skills that our young people need for success in college and careers. With American students fully prepared for the future, our communities will be best positioned to compete successfully in the global economy. (Core Standards.org, mission statement)

Clearly the authors of this statement, like Mr. Dulli more than a decade earlier, believe they know what the future will require of students.

ASSUMPTIONS: KNOWING AND REGULATING FUTURES

This common core purpose statement challenged by the arguments of Armstrong, Ohanian, Zhao, and others, clearly suggests current school policies and practices that parallel the environmental policies and practices initiated in Pinchot's Forest Service. The primary difference is that rather than stewarding natural resources, education authorities and policy makers are managing students and teaching. However, our nation's students and teachers are perhaps our greatest natural resource.

Increasingly complicated and restrictive regulations control what happens in state policy so that bureaucratic state regulators extend those policies to school districts; school board members and superintendents extend those policies to schools; principals extend them to classrooms; and teachers apply them to students. The creators of these policies and practices take for granted that they know what students will need to know for the future. Additionally, these policy makers and regulators believe that the only learning needs these students have or will have are related to their need to work.

This entire chain of events depends on three erroneous assumptions. Assumption 1 is that these modern, positivist political leaders really know what they are doing with education, as they ignore the advice of experts in education and other fields who believe that they don't. Assumption 2 is that schools are complicated organizations that can be fixed by effectively applying mechanical solutions. The third assumption is that making students and teachers accountable through a high-stakes test will motivate them to acquire the skills the policy makers and their agents have identified as necessary. Let's examine this last assumption.

THE FLAWS OF STANDARDIZED TESTS

States, districts, and schools have been collecting data, especially test data about students, for a long time. The author began his teaching career in the mid-1970s. One week each year was dedicated to achievement testing. Several hours each day were dedicated to administering standardized tests to students. At some point during the school year the school principal would get results from the tests administered during the previous year. Occasionally, he would share those results with teachers in a faculty meeting.

These were low-stakes tests and honestly useless for a teacher. Students' scores would be a bit higher or lower in each sub-test from one year to the next. However, because the scores were always a year old when received by teachers, they had no value as an assessment of students' learning needs. Those students had gone on to the next grade. Additionally, because each group of students was unique and different from the members of the previous class, they had very little value as a tool for improving instruction.

So basically, teachers did not pay much attention to them. What has changed about the tests since that time? Not much, really. Generally, scores from one year are provided to districts in the following year. Oh, but one thing is changing. Policy makers are placing increasingly high stakes bets on these tests. Consequently districts, principals, and teachers are learning to dance to the test maker's tune.

James Popham (2001), former president of the American Educational Research Association, spent much of his professional career developing standardized tests but eventually described himself as a *"recovering test developer"* (p. 75). He provided an in-depth discussion of the flaws associated with standardized testing, concluding that in most districts half or more than half of what is tested is not even in the tested grade's curriculum.

Just as importantly, the nature of standardized test construction is to create differentiation in student response. That is, the test is designed to produce an adequate number of errors. Therefore, much of what should be tested is not tested, because the vast majority of students will have learned that content, and they would get the right answers. Therefore, a test demonstrating appropriate grade level content would not differentiate among the students.

Some educators know that student differentiation is the primary function of norm-referenced tests. But many teachers, principals, and parents are under the impression that criterion-based, standards-based, or standards referenced tests are different. They mistakenly believe that these state tests are accurate measures of each student's skill or knowledge in reference to specific state standards.

However, these criterion-referenced tests were developed by the same psychometricians and companies that generate normed tests. Consequently, Popham (2001) said criticisms aimed at the national norm-referenced achievement tests can be applied to these state criterion-referenced tests as well. All achievement tests, he concluded, are designed to differentiate so that students can be grouped or sorted. They differ in that norm-referenced tests sort into percentiles or stanines, and state-based tests sort into below proficient, proficient, or some other set of group labels.

Additionally, Popham argues and virtually every experienced teacher, principal, and parent knows that student learning varies significantly from student to student, and year to year. Our children are humans, and each human is a unique and complex system. If you know someone who doesn't believe this, then ask that person to walk down a busy street with you. It is highly unlikely that you will see any two people who are alike, unless they just happen to be twins. And even then, if you look closely, you will see differences.

Popham (2001) identified two elements that make a testing program "high stakes" (p. 33). An assessment is a high-stakes assessment if

- Significant consequences are linked to individual student performance.
- Students' scores determine the instructional success or ranking of a school.

Almost all states now practice some level of high-stakes testing.

What evidence is available related to the idea that mastery of traditional lower learning skills measured by standardized tests will prepare our young for the future? Psychologist Robert Sternberg (1998) studied testing at Yale. He found that white, middle-class students from better schools tended to do very well in traditional learning and testing situations steeped in memory-analytical skills. However, these skills are not the skills most needed in work environments. He found that creative and practical skills were actually more important in work performance, whether for an administrator/manager, scientist, teacher, or artist.

Sternberg also found that students from a variety of ethnic and social backgrounds often learn and perform better in these skills areas and indeed perform better even on traditional tests when their learning occurred with an emphasis on creative and practical skills. Additionally, he found that our schools de-emphasize creative and practical skills. The focus on lower-level skills enables middle- and upper-middle class white students to perform well in the school environment. However, this does not adequately prepare these students for work.

These traditional teaching frameworks emphasizing memory-analytical skills also inhibit the success of minority and lower socioeconomic background students precisely because they do not build on the creative and practical skills that are their strengths. Sternberg found that our testing system tends to support white middle-class students at the expense of lower-income and minority students. Perhaps even more importantly, test-focused instruction works against the development of the kinds of skills that would enable all students, including white, minority, high-income, and low-income students to perform better in the workplace.

DEVELOPING HUMANS TO CREATE KNOWLEDGE

Armstrong (2006) defined "human development discourse" as "the totality of speech acts and written communications that define the purpose of education primarily in terms of supporting, encouraging, and facilitating a student's growth as a whole human being, including his or her cognitive, emotional, social, ethical, creative, and spiritual unfoldment" (p. 39). Human development discourse fits well with Maslov's hierarchy of needs, Pink's (2009) 3.0 motivation system, and the conclusions reached by Ariely (2009) regarding the mistaken emphasis on attempting to replace social norms with market norms in educational settings.

This is clearly a much broader view than academic achievement discourse. The emphasis on academic achievement discourse represents a crisis because it has virtually eliminated human development discourse. The academic achievement discourse that Armstrong described is a modern positivist view that places the student as the object of a treatment prescribed by the curriculum creator, who is someone in a position of power: state department of education personnel, textbook developer, or politician. The school and teacher are merely the instruments managed by that power source.

Human development discourse, on the other hand, places the student as a self-defining element. She or he, guided by the teacher, is capable of choosing her or his own course of development. The teacher facilitates and assists the student in that development. The self-actualizing needs of the student provide the motivation needed to develop creative abilities. This is the exact process that generates the inventive and entrepreneurial spirit children require for successful futures. Isn't this an ultimately more practical approach than the narrow focus created by academic achievement discourse?

Within human development discourse, the ultimate goal for the teacher is to enable the student's learning to go beyond what the teacher knows and, as Ariely (2009) suggested, emphasize goals designed to improve human life rather than goals that are assumed will improve test scores, which presumably improves student marketability. Most teachers cannot realize this goal during their period of interaction with the student. It is a vision: the teacher's task is teaching how to learn.

Why must this be the teacher's vision? Because the student needs to generate the new knowledge the future will require. These ideas about generating knowledge predate the modern period. In truth, these ideas enabled the modern period to occur, and they are essential ideas for the postmodern period as well. They represent the core idea of the *LTL* process. *LTL* is an ongoing exchange of information between participants engaged in leading and following that can generate new learning.

Many educational reformers would argue that the standards movement came about in response to and rejection of the open classroom, student-affirming practices of the 1960s and 1970s. The ideas of building student curiosity and self-esteem were in fact the author's primary reasons for becoming a teacher. Back then, we believed that enabling students to feel good about themselves would lead to greater motivation for learning.

Perhaps we underestimated or misinterpreted the human need for challenge: what we now call rigor. However, reflecting on the enormous growth of the American economy and the incredible advancements in science and technology in the years since strongly suggests that maybe educators were onto something. Just when and where did those young adults of the 1980s and 1990s acquire the creative abilities, system challenging, and practical skills that caused those scientific and technological transformations to occur that sparked the economic explosion?

THE REAL WHOPPER: THE FAILURE OF SCHOOLING

Perhaps you know someone who likes to tell stories that contain a certain limited veracity. These folks are continuously concerned with one-upmanship. Such an individual must tell a story that outdoes or outstretches any other story told. We often refer to these stories as fish tales. A "Whopper" story is a tale about the big one that got away. One of the great whoppers of recent history is the tale of widespread educational disaster in the United

States. It was first started back in the 1960s, sparked in response to Russia's Sputnik satellite. Unfortunately, this whopper gets bigger with each retelling. It has been such a whale of a story that it is still growing today.

Now, some of the folks cited in this section have suggested that these storytellers knowingly limit their veracity. Instead, the proposition here is that politicians, trapped in modern positivist thinking, truly believe their stories and have been extremely successful in getting others to believe them as well, which reinforces their beliefs. They are blinded by the limitations of their positivist thinking and do not know what they think they know. The following is a pragmatic interpretation of the story of the forever ongoing and continuously growing failure of schools in the United States. Let's examine this whopper story.

If you are close to the author's age you likely remember the *A Nation at Risk* (National Commission on Excellence in Education, 1983) generated by the Reagan White House. The blue-ribbon panel that developed this report began with the following introduction.

> Our Nation is at risk. Our once unchallenged preeminence in commerce, industry, science, and technological innovation is being overtaken by competitors throughout the world. This report is concerned with only one of the many causes and dimensions of the problem, but it is the one that undergirds American prosperity, security, and civility. We report to the American people that while we can take justifiable pride in what our schools and colleges have historically accomplished and contributed to the United States and the well-being of its people, the educational foundations of our society are presently being eroded by a rising tide of mediocrity that threatens our very future as a Nation and a people. What was unimaginable a generation ago has begun to occur—others are matching and surpassing our educational attainments. (National Commission on Excellence in Education, 1983, Introduction)

So, if *A Nation at Risk* was accurate, how did the fantastic economic and technological growth of the 1980s and 1990s happen? Just how did those students who were products of that rising tide of mediocrity do it? Yes, back then our weakest schools served the poor and minorities. They still do and after almost twenty years of standards development, standards-based curriculums, and increasing emphasis on standardized tests, the lives and education of children of poverty have not improved. But had the weaknesses of schools serving the poor spread to other schools? Was there really a national crisis of mediocrity?

Please know that the *Nation at Risk* report was written without any input from educators. In fact, all of the participants on the blue-ribbon panel were politicians. Indeed, most of the panel members were Republican governors interested in keeping Ronald Reagan in the White House (Ansary, 2007). The economy was faltering and they needed an issue. What could possibly be a better issue than pinning the economic ills plaguing the country on the failure of our educational system to keep up with the Japanese and Germans? After all, the nation's schools were not adept at defending themselves from attack.

The report didn't provide any real information about this supposed failure. It did, however, report one deceptive fact: Overall SAT scores had declined from 1963 through 1980. Therefore, in 1990, Admiral James Watkins, then Secretary of Energy, commissioned scientists at Sandia National Laboratories in Albuquerque to document the decline of schooling in America. That is, their assignment was to find proof of the failing schools that *A Nation at Risk* described. However, these researchers were unable to do that. Indeed, they found the opposite of what they had anticipated.

Admiral Watkins's team found that the notion of poorer school performance was false. Yes, it was true that SAT scores had steadily declined between the 1970s and the 1990s. However, because schools had been so successful in improving graduation rates for poor and minority students, the numbers of SAT test takers had risen dramatically. Many more minority, poor, and middle-income students were graduating, taking the SAT exam, and attending college (Ansary, 2007; Bracey, 2004). This was an example of Simpson's Paradox. Although overall SAT scores decreased, the results for virtually every subgroup examined by Watkins's team had improved.

How did this happen? In the 1950s and 1960s, only small numbers of students from primarily white, well-off families took the SAT. These students had always done well on tests. However, they represented a declining proportion of students taking the exam each year. Consequently, overall scores during the period went down. But scores for the white, well-off student subgroup went up, as did scores for minority and lower-income student subgroups as well.

The report from Sandia National Laboratories, in direct opposition to *A Nation at Risk*, demonstrated that the nation's schools were not failing. They were demonstrating substantial success in getting a much higher percentage of students to graduate from high school, attend college, and, as subgroups, achieve higher test scores. The report concluded that America's schools were getting better—not worse.

But by this time, the Republican Party had built this fish story into an essential part of their agenda. George H. W. Bush was running on an education reform agenda. Perhaps you are old enough to remember how he was going to be the "education president"? So the White House buried the Sandia Report. It was not published until 1993 and was circulated only among education professionals, who were largely ignored by policy makers.

Therefore, the failing schools story became such a whopper that Bill Clinton felt the need to generate an even larger reform agenda and developed Goals 2000 (1994). Then, in 1999, George W. Bush ran on an "education president" platform, which led to *No Child Left Behind* (2000), followed by Barack Obama's *Race to the Top* (2010) reforms. It seems this whopper is still in the political lake and growing bigger each election season. It also seems to have given us an endless supply of "education presidents." Also, take a look who is sitting in your state governor's chair. Odds are that you have an education governor to boot.

Clearly, *A Nation at Risk*, the numerous reports of American educational failure written since, and the resultant legislation have more to do with political opportunism than school failure. It has been almost fifty-five years since the U.S.S.R. launched Sputnik and our politicians discovered that our schools were "failing." That first iteration described how our schools had fallen behind the Russians in math and science. Then, it was the Japanese and Germans. Now we are falling behind the Chinese and Indians—the ones in India, not America. Once again, do we know what we think we know? Are we learning anything?

CAN WE BREAK OUT OF THE POSITIVIST TRAP?

Philosopher-educator Parker Palmer (1993) talked about the objective nature of our Western worldview. We see ourselves surrounded by objects that we believe are separate from us. We manipulate objects through power and coercion. We think in terms of cause and effect and ignore the possible connections between objects and ourselves, between people, and between teachers and students.

He believes that some of the new epistemologies or ways of knowing tell us that we should speak only of nature and ourselves at the same time. Palmer wrote:

> If we believed in this organic relationship of the knower and the known, we would create a classroom practice that would teach us not to rearrange the world but to learn its intricate relationships. The knower would become a person whose destiny is not to rule, but to raise to consciousness the interrelated quality of all of life, to enter into partnership with nature, history, society, and ourselves. (Palmer, 1993, p. 38)

The epistemologies Palmer described represent a higher level of knowing that is more in line with the pragmatic philosophy of John Dewey and contemporary, interpretive, qualitative, and constructivist views. The nature of the knowledge about which Palmer spoke is related to the idea of *LTL* and seeking wisdom, and very different from the modern positive-objectivist framework. The representation of these views is critical for education and our nation.

Chapter 1 discussed the application of Developmental Empowerment as a foundational part of the *LTL* framework based upon the work of Belenky, Bond, and Weinstock (1997). Their work points to "a central contradiction in our cultural heritage that has had tragic consequences for men as well as women, for children, for families, and for society as a whole—that those who do the caring work do not require, or warrant care" (Belenky et al., 1997, p. 53).

Belenky and colleagues studied the development of "voice" in disempowered women's groups by engaging the women in dialogue. They created "Epistemological Perspectives of Self and Relations with Peers and Children," a framework that demonstrates the growth of disempowered women study participants in thinking about their own thinking from being "silenced" to becoming "constructive knowers" as they participated in dialogic processes (pp. 76–77).

Belenky et al. (1997) credited Barbara Omolade with first recognizing "a tradition that has no name" as a form of leadership focused upon drawing out the leadership potential of each individual, "rooted in an ancient tradition originating in African tribal societies and organized around democratic/consensus building processes" (p. 11). They discussed the dichotomies so common in Western thought: thinking vs. feeling, nature vs. nurture, white vs. black, male vs. female. Belenky et al. documented the development of "otherness," as the self turns others into objects, clearly reflecting modern positivistic cause-effect knowledge recognition.

They discussed the traditional white male-dominated power structure of Western civilization: what is described herein as the modern positivist-objectivist point of view. They cite the work of Carol Gilligan (1982), who challenged Lawrence Kohlberg's conclusion that males develop higher levels of moral development than do females. Instead, Gilligan demonstrated that women develop very sophisticated moral structures that are focused more on human relationships than on the application of modern objective rules.

Gilligan said

> Moral problems are problems of human relations, and in tracing the development of an ethic of care, I explore the psychological grounds for nonviolent human relations. This relational ethic transcends the age-old opposition between selfishness and selflessness, which have been the staples of moral discourse. The search on the part of many people for a voice, which transcends these false dichotomies, represents an attempt to turn the tide of moral discussion from questions of how to achieve objectivity and detachment to how to engage responsively and with care. (Gilligan, 1982, p. xix)

In chapter 3, the analysis by Bellinger et al. (2004) of Ackoff's five categories of the content of the human mind was discussed. They revised the five categories into four, suggesting that Ackoff's categories can be viewed as developmental stages. They removed understanding as a category and viewed it as one of two factors that contribute to movement from one stage to the next. The other factor is connectedness.

The four stages that result are data, no understanding and no connectedness; information, an understanding that each datum is connected to other data in a specific way; knowledge, the understanding that information can be connected to other information to solve problems with a good degree of predictability; and wisdom, understanding that multiple sets of knowledge are connected but that many of those connections may be unseen. Lloyd (2006) added the idea that multiple wisdom frameworks may compete with one another.

The description by Bellinger et al. (2004) of human wisdom as the development of high levels of understanding and connection, and Lloyd's (2006) recognition of multiple wisdom frameworks parallel the newer epistemologies suggested by Palmer, the ethic of care identified by Gilligan, and the constructive knowing studied by Belenky et al. These ideas also fit with Sternberg's (2004) definition of wisdom. They suggest that a wisdom seeker aims for a level of spatial and timeless universality by seeking commonalities among competing frameworks while accepting competing and unsettled wisdom claims.

These ideas fit well with notions of wisdom that originated in the East. Chia and Holt (2007) argue that whereas the Western worldview has held that reality exists in a static form, reality in the Orient is dynamic and changing. In the West, we have thought in terms of "form, substance, essence, fullness, completeness, coherence, and finality. For the East, however, it is *nothingness, emptiness, and the undetermined that are the fecund progenerative origin—the source of potentiality for all things*" (Chia and Holt, 2007, p. 515; author's italics).

In the West, we have oriented ourselves toward mastering circumstance with power acquired through knowledge, but Eastern thought is associated with unlearning and emptying of the mind and a view of wisdom as learned ignorance. Learned ignorance, or stated another way, recognition of one's ignorance, becomes an ally for developing understanding rather than a foe to be defeated. Stated another way, recognition of ignorance is a prerequisite for learning because knowers cannot learn. An individual cannot learn what she or he already knows.

Rather than limiting an examination of what might be with our assumption of superior knowledge, a new, postmodern search for wisdom can reveal possible futures and enable the development of the requisite variety needed for participation in a society that must continually adapt. A new search for wisdom may allow for an examination of the limitations imposed by modern, positively framed objective knowledge that leads to academic achievement discourse grounded in carrots and stick motivation—which, unfortunately, is mostly sticks in education today.

The idea of wisdom as learned ignorance and understanding that we don't know what we think we know provides us with the humility needed to recognize the limits of what is known and encourages a continuous and ongoing inquiry of what is, toward what can be. Continuously questioning what seems to be true is the heart of the *LTL* framework: ongoing cycles of inquiry by individuals and groups as they strive to reach higher levels of knowing.

Seeking wisdom through *inquiry* produces an *LTL* process: a state of continuous social evolution that will enable us to address our unknown but changing future. Pursuing wisdom is leading, teaching, and learning. Wisdom seeking through *open inquiry* and *developmental empowerment* changes our framework from knowing to learning and from being to becoming.

Ultimately, wisdom seeking is a pursuit that occurs within an individual. But its potential value becomes apparent when it is done in community. It is the nature of our individual learning and recognition of our individual ignorance that enables each of us to teach others: to develop, use, and share our windows, doors, and mirrors. Parker Palmer's (1998) idea is that authentic teaching means teaching who and what we are.

We can also include the idea that each of us is becoming; each of us is evolving. If you, the author, or anyone for that matter, teach only what we know and what is known, and avoid sharing what we don't know and is not known, then we are not in a learning relationship. In fact, it becomes a learning avoidance relationship. This is the paradox: its resolution: the unique relationship among learning, teaching, and leading. A leader teaches by learning. This is the essence of *LTL*.

Chapter Five

A Different Patriotism

Our nation was founded more than 200 years ago by a group of wisdom-seeking men who, in spite of significant variations in their views, were able to come together and reach agreement around a single cause: oppression by the British Crown. Since that risky beginning, our nation has been tested many times. Usually, those tests have had clearly identifiable causes: foreign threats, disease, and economic turmoil.

To date, we have worked hard to identify and overcome such perils. We have developed a military capacity unequaled by any other nation to protect us from foreign threat. We have developed an incredible scientific and technological capacity that enables the discovery of new machines, new medicines, and although not always successful, new approaches to social and economic problems. In fact, we did recover from the Great Depression, as well as the so-called Great Malaise of the 1970s, and are now slowly recovering from what we are labeling the Great Recession.

MANAGEMENT THROUGH FEAR

However, we now face a new threat. Actually, it is a threat that has been with us all along, but one we have seldom realized. It is a complex problem that comes from within each of us: our fear. This fear is accompanied by its production correlates, anger and blame. This unrecognized threat has grown exponentially as we have developed and continue to develop more complicated machinery, greater technological competence, and increasingly fast-paced lives.

Indeed, this fear is likely what lies at the base of the conservative Tea Party populists' aims when they speak of taking America back. They seem to fear the direction toward which we are moving and want to go back to a simpler, less complex time. They are angry and place blame on anyone advocating change. Progressives, on the other hand, seem to advocate any and all change and fear those who they believe work to prevent change. But they seem to ignore a history full of lessons about changes that did not work. Peter Senge (1990) observed that every solution contains the seeds of new problems, which many progressives seem not to understand.

So, just what can we do to overcome the increasing anger, blame, and divisiveness that result from the fear so prevalent in our society? It is time for a new framing of our organizations and a different way of thinking. We need different ways of being and working together. Certainly, the way we move forward is not by going back, as the conservative populists would have us do. Neither should we jump on board every new progressive proposal.

What's needed is both a step back and a step forward. We must relearn the ancient skills of conversation. We must learn again how to inquire—how to dialogue and how to discuss. Our success depends upon our ability to develop more open, self-reflective conversational strategies than our past has ever required. We must find ways to overcome the isolation developing in our increasingly silo-like institutions. Either we come together or we fall apart.

Generally, in America today, we talk at or out-yell one another. Try listening to programming on Fox News, MSNBC, or even CNN. Worse yet, just try to listen to almost anything on commercial talk radio. We need to relearn respectful listening, redevelop the openness to ideas with which each of us was born, and learn to speak with our own voice, understanding that we are each presenting our individual truth while recognizing that others may know a different truth.

We need to have a method of civil, multi-path communication serving as a primary focus of organizational and cross-organizational existence: a respectful way to inquire into others' views and an openness to accept conflicting presentations of reality as opportunities for developing new truths. Actually, what is advocated here is learning: pursuing wisdom in creating new knowledge. Without learning, our nation will decline. With learning, we will continue to thrive.

However, we have a leadership problem. Who can provide the leadership needed to address and alleviate our fear? Where in our society are we most capable of having this learning occur? Who in our society is capable of guiding the inquiry that will enable this learning to occur? Where will we find a leadership model that will guide us to develop the agreements upon which to build our future?

Our nation's founders created a government founded on balancing political and social power. They created a constitution to create an organization that balances power between the central government and its original thirteen member states. This organization also divided power between an executive, a legislative, and a judicial branch. Each of these branches had specific powers over the other branches of the organization. But no one branch of this government contained enough power to usurp the powers of the other two branches.

The founders wrote this constitution guaranteeing certain powers to each of the member states, certain powers to each of the three branches, and, by adding ten initial amendments to this document, guaranteed certain rights to the individuals in each of the member states. This constitution created an organization called the United States that has survived and thrived for two centuries.

Unfortunately, the internal threat of fear that drives so many of the nation's individual members, and that threatens the national organization's existence, was not addressed in our founding document. The balancing characteristics of the constitution were based on a belief in individual enterprise and competition. This worked because the organizing culture of the founders was based on reason, openness, and civility, resulting in collaboration and cooperation: the characteristics of open inquiry.

How else can we account for the Constitution? The founders had experimented with a very weak limited confederation of states for eight years after the end of the Revolution. Even with their strongly held differences, they were able to get along with one another at the Constitutional Convention because they recognized the necessity for so doing: the need for unity to overcome external threats and establish processes for working together.

Do we still have the ability to come together, as the nation's founders did? We certainly did so in each of the world wars. On more recent occasions, we have banded together to address external threats, including the terrorist attack on September 11, 2001. What remains to be seen, however, is whether we have the ability to come together to face our current and increasingly more dangerous internal threat: our fear. From where will the leadership come that brings us together so that we understand and address this fear?

Traditionally, we have looked to Washington, our state houses, and city hall for leadership. But presidents, congressmen, governors, and mayors are not leaders. They are followers who choose their words and behaviors to appeal to enough citizens to acquire new or maintain current elected positions. That is, they claim to lead, but instead they follow the people, and this is as it should be in a democracy. Indeed, British Prime Minister Benjamin Disraeli once said, "I must follow the people, am I not their leader" (Benjamin Disraeli Quotes.mht).

Every politician running for any office proclaims that she or he will provide the leadership the electorate needs. However, our politicians are competitively oriented and think in terms of winning and losing. They talk of leadership, but are seldom capable of exhibiting it. They are managers who seek to control opinions and outcomes to support their own success. But many are not doing this well. Indeed, recent opinion polls suggest that Congressional approval ratings are now approaching single digits. Frankly, our politicians cannot provide the leadership model and practices our society needs to adapt to the future.

At one time, we had highly respected news media professionals in whom we placed great trust. Media leaders like Walter Cronkite, Chet Huntley, and David Brinkley spoke as centralizing forces. Indeed, President Johnson chose to end his political career after hearing Walter Cronkite express his disagreement with the Vietnam War. He said, "If I've lost Cronkite, I've lost middle America" (CBS News Video).

However, these highly respected media leaders no longer exist. Today, we have networks dedicated entirely to news production, where media professionals make increasingly outrageous appeals to narrow sets of interest. Clearly, these networks produce rather than report news. These folks are in the news creation business; as the news production sources multiply, the narrowness of interest representation increases, appealing to small audiences, who only communicate with other members of their silo groups.

Often, these media personalities refer to themselves as commentators and even entertainers. They compete for television viewer market share and focus on sensationalism to keep their viewers engaged in their programming. In essence, they are selling fear, anger, and blame. Present-day media broadcasters and pundits have invented a new tribalism and are certainly not going to lead the conversations we need to bring us together.

Some individuals look to the business sector for the leadership we need. Indeed, we have historically had periods in our history when successful businessmen have been lionized as models of leadership. This remains a dominant view as several extremely successful individuals are still idolized. But where were the lions of business who should have provided the guidance that would have prevented our recent economic calamity?

Where were the Wall Street leaders prior to the stock market collapse? Where were the leaders of the mortgage-banking sector who could have prevented the housing industry collapse? These folks were at least partially responsible for these calamities. Were they blinded by greed? Were they blind to reality? Clearly, they did not know what they thought they knew. The business sector does not have the capacity to lead the learning we need.

So, who is left? The ministry? The religious history of the United States can be viewed as a process of multiplying religious denominations based on disagreement and dispute. The author's local phone book serves an area of less than half a million people. It contains multiple church listings for a large variety of denominations including Adventists, Apostolistics, Anglicans, and Assemblies of God. Those are just the denominations beginning with the letter A. There are listings for 320 churches representing Baptists, including

Free Will Baptists, Independent Baptists, Missionary Baptists, and Southern Baptists.

Many of these churches and church denominations claim that theirs is the "true" church. Which church might the gentleman described in chapter 3, who was driving the luxury automobile with the "truth is not relative" bumper sticker attend? Members of the clergy are not likely to lead the collaborative processes needed to bring us together. In fact, some of them are as engaged in promoting fear as are the media experts.

A NEW LEADERSHIP MODEL

Who in our society models the collaboration needed to allow diverse human beings to reach agreements about purpose and tasks? There seems to be only one realistic place to look: the schools. Our schools have been looked down upon as dismal organizational failures. However, our schools are the only American institutions that continually focus on finding common ground among diverse groups. Historically, educators have believed that their work is not political. Schooling has always been at the whim of those who wield power so that educator career success has been dependent upon jumping on political bandwagons.

But more than thirty years of work as a teacher, principal, and professor has led to the conclusion that this is wrong. Now, recent economic and political events, as unfortunate as they have been, have generated the courage to challenge the failing schools myth and a hope that the message might be heard. Today, most people rate their local schools more highly than their governments, banks, mortgage companies, automobile manufacturers, health insurers, firms that provide the nation with food and commodities, news media outlets, and other people's churches.

It is true, as discussed in a chapter 3, that there are many schools serving students of poverty, where teachers and principals face odds strongly stacked against student and school success—schools where disempowered, worn out, and inexperienced teachers are caught in vicious cycles of the failure and blame so dominant in our nation. However, they are not representative of most schools in America, although all schools are victimized by contemporary political policies and economic practices that generate those cycles of failure and blame.

Right now in most neighborhoods, the schools are successful organizations in spite of receiving the blame for many or perhaps most of our society's problems. Peter Schrag, analyzing patterns of school reform in the United States, discussed how political "rhetoric has loaded virtually all social problems on the school, as if there were no other social institutions and no need to provide them" (Schrag, 2004, p. 360). Consequently, schools have been the subject of one failed quick fix after another (Fullan and Hargreaves, 1996). Schrag calls this an "orgy of reform" (Schrag, 2004, p. 359).

Yet, most of our schools have survived years of policies designed to fix them and somehow continued to thrive. This is because our schools, especially our elementary schools, have become natural learning organizations that are worthy of study and emulation, not only by other schools but by other organizations as well. Most schools have learned to meet the needs of increasingly diverse student populations through generations of often-misguided policy fixes and expanding social responsibilities, while maintaining stable, ordered environments and meeting their primary organizational goals: teaching students to be successful citizens, workers, and learners.

Despite the whopper myths about a failed education system generated by so many politicians and media pundits, most schools in the United States are getting better and have been doing so for quite some time. A recent report advocating school turnaround strategies quotes U.S. Department of Education Statistics that 5 percent of our schools are failing and suggests that this number could double within the next five years (*The School Turnaround Field Guide*, 2010). However, this report does not focus on the 90–95 percent of schools that have continued to be successful.

Even so, we should be very concerned about the 5–10 percent of failing schools and finding ways to address their needs. Between 1999 and 2000, and 2007 and 2008, the number of high poverty schools has increased from 15 percent to 20 percent for elementary schools and from 5 percent to 9 percent for secondary schools (NCES, 2010). However, these statistics don't demonstrate that our schools are failing. Schools do not impoverish people.

A more accurate portrayal is that our social and economic systems are failing increasing numbers of our children and that our schools have been doing a wonderful job in attempting to minimize the negative impacts of our failing social and economic systems. After all, our nation is better educated today than ever before. The number of twenty-five- to twenty-nine-year-olds who completed a bachelor's degree jumped from 17 percent in 1971 to 29 percent in 2009 (National Center for Educational Statistics [NCES], 2010).

So maybe it is time for organizational theorists, economists, news analysts, pundits, and politicians to look at schools as successful organizations and models worthy of emulation. After all, the corporations, many of which are failing or have failed, have been presented as models for schools to emulate for many years. You might attempt to count the number of candidates running for your local school board who argue that schools should be run more like businesses. Perhaps it is time to run our businesses and other organizations more like schools. Maybe political, business, religious, and other leaders need to emulate principals and teachers.

Certainly our schools are not perfect organizations. As the department of education reported, one in twenty of our schools is failing. But many of our schools, our best schools, are much better representatives of the learning organizations that business and market system advocates claim to represent. Our educators may be the real leaders in our society, and they seem to have been quietly leading for many years.

A New Testament proverb suggests that a prophet is not recognized in his own land (Biblio.com, 2004). This is likely true for organizations as well. What could a small neighborhood organization, like a school, possibly have to share with government or large corporations? This chapter will describe some of those practices, behaviors, and thinking processes. But politicians, corporate heads, and the experts who advise them may not be able to see something so close and visible.

Maybe it is time for us to look in our local neighborhoods for the models of organization that can help our society develop solutions to regional, national, and global problems. After all, organization theorist Peter Senge talked about the "art of seeing the forest and the trees" (Senge, 1990, p. 127). A book chapter by management professor Robert Rowden (2008) entitled "The Learning Organization and Strategic Change" clearly makes the case.

FOUR PHASES OF STRATEGIC PLANNING

Rowden (2008), writing from a business leadership perspective, suggested that the idea of learning organizations came about in response to the limitations of previous top-down strategic change models. He outlined four phases in the evolution of organizational strategic planning and presented learning organizations as the fourth phase. The first version, developed during the 1940s and 1950s, emphasized formal planning based upon the objective analysis of quantitative data and top-down management. Such strategic planning can be labeled as fixing the machines.

During the 1970s, a second phase of strategic planning recognized that change strategies alone were insufficient and that detailed execution of strategic plans needed to include middle management in the development of implementation plans. You might think of this phase as fixing the factory line operators. The third phase placed an emphasis on developing readiness to change in response to organizational barriers such as employee resistance and other unanticipated problems that delayed or prevented the success of change initiatives, or fixing unhappy workers.

The description Rowden (2008) provided for each of these phases suggests a gradual evolution in the modern positivist, mechanical framework toward greater involvement of organizational participants. These phases appeared to be increasingly democratic, but always depended upon acceptance of centrally mandated ideas. Each subsequent phase reveals a wider involvement of organizational participants but always as objects of top management–driven centralized reform.

In each of these three phases of strategic planning, organizational participants are consumers of management ideas and not agents acting within the organization. The basic leadership assumption was always that superordinates have superior knowledge that they can and should use to solve organizational problems. In essence, each phase represented an effort to "sell" solutions to broader groups of the organization's participants. Organization leaders believed that all they needed was to get "buy-in" from participants.

These phases have had enormous effects on our schools. School principal involvement first appears in the second phase. Teacher involvement is evident during the third phase, but tied to implementing strategic initiatives developed at the school system level or by an ambitious principal. Experienced teachers and principals are very aware of strategic planning, as they have experienced phases two and three in the development of school and school district improvement plans by state direction and recently by federal mandate. As a result, many and perhaps most schools are trapped in an endless succession of magic bullet cures.

Therefore, the common theme heard among school leaders today is "We need to get buy-in" for the latest magic bullet available. However, a wise friend once told the author that "You can always buy, but you can't always sell." Teachers, it seems, have become increasingly better shoppers. They are buying into less and less of what is out there in the education magic bullet shop. Teachers are realizing that the bag of carrots offered to them increasingly contains the sharp sticks of accountability.

In contrast to the "buy-in" strategies of the first three phases, the primary idea of a learning organization is that planning and leadership are spread widely throughout the organization (Senge, 1990; O'Toole, 2008). In other words, the organization's participants engage in *LTL* relationships. All of the participants are practitioners in leading, teaching, and learning as engaged agents representing the organization, rather than merely customers for central or top leaders' solution products.

Participants in *LTL* relationships are agents who have both a right and a responsibility to participate in the leadership of the organization. Therefore, contained within the idea of the learning organization is a quality of democratic organizational participation: not just an image of democracy that presents itself once the participant has "bought in." Democratic responsibility provides the learning organization with the requisite variety the organization needs to continually adapt to environmental change.

Democratic responsibility is the common cultural practice of good schools and is how our schools have successfully survived and thrived in spite of many years of misguided reform. Rowden (2008) provided an excellent framework that identifies the characteristics of a learning organization. These characteristics are process keys that extend leadership throughout the organization. He was writing primarily about the learning organization characteristics of business organizations. However, his description of learning organization characteristics is an accurate portrait of our best schools.

GOOD SCHOOLS: REAL LEARNING ORGANIZATIONS

Rowden (2008) identified six characteristics common to learning organizations:

1. They *provide continuous learning opportunities.*
2. They *use learning to reach their goals.*
3. They *link individual performance with organizational performance.*
4. They *foster inquiry and dialogue*, making it safe for people to share openly and take risks.
5. They *embrace creative tension* as a source of energy and renewal.
6. They are continuously *aware and interact with their environment* (Rowden, 2008, p. 285).

These six characteristics are clearly embodied in good schools. For example, the primary purpose of the school is to *provide continuous learning opportunities* for students; teachers *use learning to reach goals* for themselves through professional staff development, so that the primary purpose can be realized.

Additionally, good schools *link individual performance to organizational performance* through the development and application of the school's vision and mission. The teacher's job is to help every student be successful; the principal's job is to help every teacher be successful. Therefore, success for each student, each teacher, and the entire school is defined by the school's mission and its movement toward the vision.

Principals and teachers in good schools *embrace creative tension,* the gap between current reality and individual or group vision of what can or should be true in the future. This gap serves as the spark for the inventive and inquiring leadership that moves toward a reframing that develops shared meaning that can transcend and close or narrow this gap (Burns, 2008; Senge, 1990).

For the teacher there is such a gap between student knowledge and the teacher's vision of what the student could know and be able to do. For the principal, there is a similar gap between teacher practice and potential, and another gap between available resources and recognized need. These tensions are addressed creatively as principals and teachers reframe their thinking, then design and take actions to address these gaps.

Participants in good schools are certainly *aware of and interact with their environment(s)*. A clear marker of a good school is parental and community involvement. When visiting a good school, you will find it difficult to tell where the school/organization ends and the community/environment begins. This is because parents and community volunteers are consistently found throughout the building engaged in a wide variety of activities with students, teachers, principal(s), and each other.

The fourth item in the list, foster inquiry and dialogue, was intentionally saved for discussion last. This aspect of a learning organization is the anchor upon which all other elements depend—one that moves a school from being a good school to being an excellent school. The quality and nature of communication is crucial because leadership in a learning organization extends throughout all parts of the organization and is the process through which change occurs (Ellinor and Gerard, 1998; Isaacs, 1999b; Lambert et al., 1995; Wheatley, 2006).

EXCELLENT SCHOOLS FOSTER INQUIRY AND DIALOGUE

In addition to the six common characteristics outlined above, Rowden presents four "defining characteristics" of the learning organization. They are "constant readiness, continuous planning, improvised implementation and action learning" (Rowden, 2008, p. 291). These four characteristics represent the difference between good and excellent schools. They allow for the learning necessary for substantial change to occur—or as Michael Fullan (2001) has argued, from existence as a superficial learning community to a deep professional learning community.

These four defining characteristics are the primary hoped-for outcomes of organizational communication and they can only occur in a group culture grounded in democratic open inquiry: practices commonly found in our best schools. This quality of open communication provides the relational patterns enabling the school's participants to move forward together rather than pulling apart.

This communication quality is appropriately identified as the *LTL* triad that other organizations and their participants can learn to emulate. The *LTL* processes of communicating through *open inquiry* designed to foster the *developmental empowerment* of participants is also the communication framework that mediocre and failing schools can strive to emulate to improve student and adult learning.

Open inquiry requires the review and questioning of current practice, framed by professional moral and ethical responsibility, so that participants/agents who provide the democratic leadership for the organization are continually working to understand and face new challenges. These conversations about the fundamental ways of "doing school" lead to new directions, new ways of thinking, and new ways of behaving (Lambert, 1999).

Such conversations depend on individuals openly sharing beliefs and concerns, in an atmosphere that challenges participants' thinking, but not their sense of well-being, and in a culture of cooperation and support rather than competition (Ellinor and Gerard, 1998). It depends on a balance between dialogue and productive discussion (Isaacs, 1999a; 1999b). As presented in chapters 1 and 2, and to be discussed more deeply in chapter 7, dialogue is conversation designed to surface the thinking of participants, and productive discussion is the practice of building and creating solutions based upon the collaborative examination of those ideas.

Participants in open inquiry learn to suspend their beliefs about their individual opinions and their assumptions about the opinions of others. Questions are accepted and appreciated by organizational participants as reflective guides for enhancing individual and group performance. Open inquiry is a requirement for the emergence of a common vision and mission to which all organizational members are dedicated, because they have each had a part in developing the vision and mission. This process promotes individual change and organizational evolution. Let's examine each of these defining characteristics.

CONTINUALLY READY FOR CHANGE

Continuous readiness is the precursor to the change process. Rowden said a learning organization is "attuned to its environment and willing to question fundamental ways of doing business" (Rowden, 2008, p. 291). Burns (2008) suggested that this questioning is a reframing process grounded in working to reduce the gap between value-based practices and a realization of an emerging reality that challenges those practices.

In the learning organization, this questioning is widely spread among the organization's participants. Principals and teachers must be ready to the point that they have learned to be proactive in reactive environments. Each year, schools receive new accountability directives that must be accommodated. Every day the school principal makes multiple decisions with little or no time for analysis. Teachers must redefine their instruction to accommodate the learning needs of students on a minute-by-minute basis.

At times, a principal must challenge or help a teacher challenge that teacher's beliefs or practices. Sometimes, a teacher or a group of teachers must challenge a principal's prior decisions, practices, or beliefs. At times, an individual school or a group of schools must challenge the policies and practices of the school district. Additionally, there are times when challenges from central office are necessary to bring about change at the school level.

Such leadership challenges are necessary and appropriate if they always have a focus on improving learning and teaching, based upon creative tension: the gap between current reality and the vision/mission of the school or district. The challenged teacher knows that the principal is working to help him improve his teaching. The challenged principal listens deeply and openly accepts helpful criticism because she understands that the teacher(s) are truly interested in helping improve the school. Central office continually scans the schools for the feedback needed to make the policy corrections that remove obstacles and enable participants in each of the district's schools to improve their work with students.

CONTINUOUS PLANNING FOR CHANGE

In most organizations and many schools, a new challenge seldom surfaces in a way that can be successfully addressed. Instead the challenge festers and grows like a cancerous tumor because people who realize the danger don't feel safe in acknowledging and surfacing that danger. They know the messenger might be killed. The open communication practices in excellent schools surface difficult questions so that potential tumors are addressed before they pose major threats.

Likewise, the creativity of each organizational participant surfaces so that capacity for change and improvement grows. Organizational planning is never finished. It is a product of collaborative informal networks that Kotter (1996; 2002) has described as important sources of organizational leadership. Such plans are open, flexible, and evolve over time. They are, as Rowden says, "embraced by the whole organization" because they are jointly developed by the participants (Rowden, 2008, p. 291).

Continuous planning makes continuous readiness possible. The principal, faculty, staff, parents, and students are in proactive decision-making positions because they have the thinking behind the plans in their hearts and heads. They know what is right in the context of the school. Additionally, when they face new questions and challenges, they know where to turn for support and assistance in modifying plans and actions.

The students, teachers, parents, and principal(s) become smarter as individuals and as a group. This occurs as a natural consequence of their *LTL* practices in democratic inquiry focused upon developing the empowerment of participants. Continuous planning is an ongoing, informal, adaptive process of communication for leading and teaching one another that enables the organization's participants to learn, and, because the participants are together, the organization learns.

IMPLEMENTATION IS IMPROVISATION

In the learning organization, plans are not implemented in an exact step-by-step fashion. Because circumstances are continuously changing, planning must be continuous, and the implementation of plans must be improvised. "[E]very member" of the organization "is a strategic planner," who acts "in creative and autonomous ways to interpret the strategic direction" (Rowden, 2008, p. 291).

Indeed, every good teacher improvises daily: sometimes revisiting an area of instruction; sometimes accelerating instruction to meet the needs of specific students; sometimes bird walking into an unplanned topical area to capitalize on intense student interest. Of course, in the best classrooms, these topical bird walks are frequently not standards based. Instead, they extend around, over, and beyond the standardized curriculum and expand the requisite variety of student knowledge. These activities enable students to imagine future possibilities.

LEARNING IN AND FROM ACTION

In a learning organization, "learning is not something that just happens. It is made to happen" (Rowden, 2008, p. 292). Participants who practice inquiry generate their own constant readiness and provide continuous organizational planning, allowing improvised implementation to occur. Learning is the product of inquiry. This is akin to the notion of *reflection in action* described by Schon (2007). It is learning from action. Often these actions are based upon tacit professional knowledge that is sometimes revealed to the actor as an outcome of learning through acting.

O'Toole (2008) studied strategic leadership in conjunction with the World Economic Forum. He was surprised to discover that the performance of large successful corporations could not be explained by traditional leadership views. He discovered a *shared leadership* where many leadership tasks were not performed by high-profile organizational heads, but rather institutionalized in the practices and cultures of the organization. Like teachers, those corporate shared leadership practitioners are the *LTL* agents of their organizations.

Action learning is common practice in excellent schools. Every classroom instructional event, faculty meeting, leadership team meeting, parent-teacher organization meeting, parent-teacher conference, student and teacher conference, and teacher visit over lunch in the lounge are opportunities for action learning. Action learning can occur whenever an individual shares information, ideas, concerns, fears, hopes, successes, and failures related to teaching and learning.

An event of sharing may spark another idea, empathy, common dreams, possibilities, or suggestions for help from the listener. Such events often lead to action by the participants: an effort to solve a problem or inspiration to pursue a new idea. However, such sharing depends upon trust. Every organizational participant must have a deep unshakable trust in other organization members. Therefore, participants in learning organizations depend upon their designated leaders in very special ways.

THE LEARNING PRINCIPAL: TRUSTED TO SERVE

Leaders in learning organizations are not necessarily the most intelligent, most inspirational, or the most charismatic of people, although many have such characteristics. However, they have one essential quality that enables their institutions to be learning organizations. They are trusted. Learning organizations cannot exist without *LTL*. *LTL* cannot exist without a high degree of trust among the organization's participants. Principals in the best schools are trusted by students, parents, teachers, community members, peers at other schools, and central office.

At one level, this trust depends upon consistency and fairness. Students, parents, and teachers know that their principal will make informed decisions and consistently follow through on them, so that there are few surprises. However, at another level, students, parents, and most importantly teachers trust that, above all else, the principal values them and their contributions to the school, more so than even the principal's own personal interests. This is a central feature in the notion of servant leadership: the leader serves the members of the organization.

The principal expects that important and sometimes hard questions will be asked and disagreements aired. These disagreements are the ingredients necessary for surfacing creative tension and a prerequisite for organizational learning. Making such disagreements visible and discussable is the hard work that leads to deep change and a responsibility for all organization participants. These disagreements surface as participants ask open honest questions (Palmer, 2004).

These questions are not designed to foster a personal agenda or provide advice in disguise, but are questions for which the inquirer truly does not have, and he wants an answer. If a teacher, parent, or student cannot question a practice or decision for the good of a student or the school, then the principal's and the school's ability to learn are limited. That is, the school is simply not a learning organization.

Open, honest questioning must be an expectation for the leader and all others in a learning organization. Such leaders do not see challenging questions as threats, but as *LTL* opportunities to increase the understanding, knowledge, and wisdom of the leader and the organization. At times, these open, honest questions may even challenge school board and/or superintendent views or polices. Principals in learning organizations risk asking these questions on behalf of their schools and, in effective school districts, get open, honest answers.

EXCELLENT PRINCIPALS MODEL OPEN INQUIRY

Quinn (2005) identified leader openness as one of four qualities leading to fundamental leadership that elevates the performance of others. Principals of excellent schools listen deeply to concerns and questions. This openness encourages the risk taking that is necessary for any substantial change to occur. Openly inquiring principals temporarily suspend their own views concerning issues while listening to the views of others as a way to gain greater insight into the understanding of other school participants.

They take time to reflect upon the ideas and suggestions they receive. They ask questions designed to enhance their understanding rather than questions designed to trap or trick the questioner. These principals also know that so doing models the teaching needed so that others may exhibit openness to learning. Often, they gain insight into a problem or issue and become convinced that a change is appropriate.

At times, the price for that insight is the realization of an error and acknowledgment that "I was wrong." This is the acid test for the principal of an excellent school: the ability to model self-reflection and honest personal analysis. If the principal can be wrong, then it is safe for others to take the risks necessary for improvement, and it is safe for others to accept and acknowledge their own errors. This can also be the acid test for school superintendents and school board members.

Actually, this is the acid test for any leader. All leaders make mistakes. How a leader responds to a mistake provides the informal process that serves as the model for organizational development and change. It is how the leader becomes a responsible agent for generating organizational learning and explains why politicians and others generally represent poor examples of leadership. This gets to the core of evolutionary learning in organizations and is a key feature of the postmodern leadership proposed as *LTL*. This test is how a leader confirms that the goal of leadership is individual and organizational learning.

TEACHERS: THE LEARNING LEADERS

Sergiovanni (2008) writes about organizational elements that substitute for leadership in schools. These substitutes include a view of the school as a community rather than an organization, and an ideal professionalism grounded in a commitment to the practice of teaching. This commitment to the practice of teaching has two levels: a teacher's commitment to improve individual teaching practice, and a commitment to improving the practice of all teachers. Sergiovanni's leadership substitutes are what others refer to as the shared leadership that occurs in a learning organization.

These so-called substitutes for leadership or shared leadership are natural qualities that good teachers bring to the profession. These commitments to improve the work of the individual and the work of the organization as a whole provide an appropriate definition of a professional. Such qualities of personal commitment extend well beyond the requirements of accountability to others. They are acceptance of individual moral and ethical responsibility.

These natural shared leadership qualities can be found in most human beings and exist in most organizations, but are either ignored or suppressed. The expression of these qualities is simply beyond the understanding of the modern positivist. After all, a mere worker could not possibly act professionally. Such a worker would need to have an area for which she or he is responsible and be trusted to make decisions related to that responsibility. The positivist believes these activities belong to managers, not followers. Such organizations have no room for leadership, especially shared leadership.

Senge et al. (1999) discussed three kinds of leaders in a learning organization: the executive leader, viewed as the head of an organization, line leaders, and network leaders. Line leaders are those individuals who drive organizational change from the front lines of an organization. This seems very similar to the work of excellent teachers who, as Sergiovanni (2007) suggests, apply scientific knowledge about teaching and professional knowledge acquired from understanding themselves as individuals in the context of the classroom, to inform the development of their professional authority and practice.

Some teachers are content being line leaders, continuously working to improve their teaching. They don't extend their leadership beyond their individual classrooms. That is just fine. These teachers dedicate themselves to providing their students with the best learning opportunities. They continue to learn about their craft and improve their teaching practices throughout their careers.

However, these teachers, because they are responsible agents and not merely accountable workers, are very selective about the choices they make in regard to their teaching practices. They will often comply with mandated changes while they are in vogue, but for the long term, only adopt those changes that they believe will improve student learning within the context of their classrooms (Tye, 2000). This responsible ability of teachers to make choices about the appropriateness of mandates is a strength that has enabled the best schools to survive misguided mandates.

The network leader informally develops connections within and across organizational boundaries (Senge, 1990). Teachers who are network leaders connect with other teachers, parents, and the community. They are the creative individuals who generate the possibilities that often lead to new grade level, school level, and district level endeavors. These network leaders are truly unrecognized heroes in schools.

In the mid-1990s, the author was a second-year principal. A general education teacher and a special education teacher presented the idea of team teaching to create an inclusive multi-age, special education, and general education classroom. They wanted to put all categories of kids with all sorts of differences into one classroom. These teachers viewed the range and variety of students' skills, interests, and talents as assets upon which they could build a successful learning community.

These two teachers were so very passionate about the possibilities that the author made certain they had the opportunity to develop their program. Four years later, half of the classes in the school were team taught, multi-age, full inclusion enterprises, each a product of the requests of teachers and parents, never the product of mandate. Throughout this transition, standardized test scores increased in these classes each year, while the scores from more traditional classrooms remained stagnant. Please note that these observations about test scores were not shared with anyone at that time so that teachers would not feel pressured to focus on test scores.

The changes initiated by these two teachers represent an event of double loop learning (Argyris and Schon, 1996), resulting in changes "in the values of theory in use, as well as strategies and assumptions" (p. 20). These two young teachers had a vision of a classroom that valued service, collaboration, and diversity, rather than entitlement, competition, and similarity, as routes to successful student learning.

They had a vision of a classroom focused on learning how to learn. Younger students in this class learned to value the knowledge of and assistance of older, more capable students and worked to emulate them. The older students developed a sense of servant leadership. These older students also discovered that if you really want to learn something, teach it to someone else. These students also disallowed bullying; they, like their teachers, became responsible agents.

One second-grade parent literally begged that her child be assigned to this classroom. After three days of school, she requested a change to a traditional classroom. Her child, she said, was working too hard and was upset that she was unable to perform like the third- and fourth-grade students. This parent was asked to wait two weeks before a change would be made. She returned one week later, saying that a transfer was no longer necessary. Her child was becoming successful in handling the challenges of the multi-age class and developing a sense of herself as a learner. This parent had learned to allow her child to accept responsibility for learning.

Among the network leaders in schools are the teachers who mentor new teachers and guide the development of professional knowledge among groups of teachers. One such teacher, in only her second year of teaching, was concerned about two first-year teachers who expressed fear about their weaknesses in successfully managing their classrooms. After a strategy session, this second-year teacher began to observe the beginners and suggest changes they could make to improve. This teacher and the two teachers she assisted went on to follow the initial multi-age visionaries and developed their own successful, collaborative, multi-age programs.

In another school, the author encountered a very experienced teacher, respected for her service to the school and community. She generated a program that made gifted education opportunities available for all students in the school. Any student could meet with this teacher to identify an idea for an independent study, develop a plan, and complete the study. This teacher had a vision of a school where every student would have opportunities to pursue learning in areas and topics for which he or she had an affinity—that is, an interest or a strength. For many students, these activities provided the engagement that made their elementary careers a success.

The author has had the honor of working with dozens of line leader and network leader teachers. Such leadership often takes courage. Sometimes it means the teacher risks the discovery that she or he is disregarding mandates to do what is right. At times, teacher leaders must challenge district policies or administrative mandates representing politically preferred techniques that attempt to limit the quality of their *LTL*.

As a new assistant principal, the author tried to prevent teachers from teaching phonics to children learning to read because the district had mandated a whole language focus. These teachers secretly continued to integrate phonics into their instruction because they tacitly knew that some students learned best through this approach. Years later it became common to observe teachers seamlessly integrating phonics into their whole language instructional framework.

Recalling previous efforts to eliminate phonics instruction, the author realized that our best teachers must sometimes disregard and even sabotage policy in order to do their work in a morally responsible way. Those teachers who, years earlier, had courageously continued to honor their tacit knowledge and use phonics instruction in their teaching of reading had been correct to do so. They placed responsibility above accountability.

These ideas about teacher leaders and learning organizations are not new. Dewey (1916) recommended that we "generate methods of utilizing the energies of human beings in accord with serious and thoughtful conceptions of life" and suggested that "Education is a laboratory in which philosophic distinctions become concrete and are tested" (p. 329). Tye (2000) wrote about factors that prevent change in schools. She quoted Wilford Aiken, the director of the Eight Year Study completed in 1942. Aiken said, "No school is ready to advance until teachers have a sure sense of security in adventure" (Tye, 2000, p. 140).

It is truly amazing that for the past 100 or so years educators have had clear images of what we now describe as learning organizations. What is perhaps even more astounding is that many schools have developed as testing laboratories and maintained a sense of adventure throughout phase after phase of political pressure and business influence designed to create more limiting organizational structural forms that squash experimentation and replace risk taking with fear. What would our nation be like if these teachers had not done so? Imagine what it will be like if they no longer do so.

SCHOOLS ARE BEACONS OF HOPE

You have read this far, so perhaps you see some truthfulness in the ideas presented and are understanding schools in a new way. After years of entrapment in an antiquated organizational and policy structure, our best schools have survived and surprisingly continue to thrive. They are not failed organizations. Instead, they are beacons for hope. If our best schools truly are valuable learning organization models, then of what value is this finding and to whom is it of value? Here are three possibilities.

First, in this post-Enron, post–mortgage-crisis era of investment house collapse, auto manufacturers' bankruptcy, Ponzi schemers, bank failures, job loss for many, increased profits for a few, and slow recovery from the Great Recession, it is clear that our political and business sectors need guidance.

We'll never know how outcomes may have differed if these organizations had modeled themselves after our best schools and developed a sense of professional responsibility.

Throughout these failed organizations, questions would have certainly been raised about the sustainability of the production of large gas-guzzling automobiles; making exorbitant loans to individuals for mortgages without verifying ability to repay; and the creation of derivative investments that created large profits for a few and huge losses for many, but seemed to have little if any value to the nation's economy and citizens.

Our best schools have a great deal that they can teach the private and political sectors about how to be as organizations in our world. They really are focused on learning, service, and continuous improvement: words frequently articulated by learning organization theorists, corporate heads, and politicians, but clearly misunderstood. Our best schools also have an abundance of what seems to be primary missing elements in much of the private and political zones: a living ethical mission and a moral vision that is not just a slogan posted upon a wall.

Sergiovanni (2007) borrowed the ideas of German sociologist Ferdinand Tönnies regarding two general types of human associations: Gemeinschaft and Gesellschaft. Gemeinschaft or community may exist in three forms: community of kinship, community of place, and community of mind. Sergiovanni said schools should be communities of place and mind where relationships are based "on what is shared and on the emerging web of obligations [that] embody that which is shared" (p. 105).

Gesellschaft relationships, on the other hand, are based upon contracts and displays of surface politeness, but in reality "everyone is thinking of himself and trying to bring to the fore his importance and advantages in competition with the others" (p. 107). The results of Ariely's (2009) research on social and market norms and consequent irrational behavior parallel Tönnies's idea of Gemeinschaft and Gesellschaft.

Sergiovanni argues that schools need to emphasize a strong sense of Gemeinschaft. Our best schools have been able to maintain this sense of community. How might outcomes have been different at Enron or more recently on Wall Street, if organizational cultures had been grounded in Gemeinschaft and deliberated on the questions of those who had the courage and integrity to voice their challenges to organizational practices rather than marginalizing and excluding their participation in the organization? Perhaps more of these organizations would have survived.

Is it time for our country to emphasize social norms that support the responsibility occurring naturally in schools rather than market norms of accountability grounded in greed? Is it possible for contemporary America to see its schools as models operating on the cusp of effective and appropriate organizational practice and modeling professional responsibility grounded in nurture and care?

Let's send our current business people, politicians, and those aspiring to be like them back to school. How about requiring them to spend some quality time observing, volunteering, and interning in our best schools? They can learn about caring, responsibility, and purpose. They can also learn about improvising to address great and still growing challenges with minimal resources in a policy atmosphere that, despite its positive intent, attempts to limit the natural learning organization attributes of schools.

Second, let's stop blaming our schools for everything that is wrong with the country. Let's develop a more realistic perspective and recognize the successes our schools have had and continue to have. However, this does not mean that principals and teachers of good schools can now sit back and say "OK, we have arrived." They know their work is never done. If the author's interpretation of Rowden's and others' frameworks for learning organizations is an accurate description of your neighborhood school, then congratulations! Your school is an example of an institution in the vanguard of human organization practice.

So, please share this chapter with the students, faculty, staff, and parents as a way to celebrate. Then let teachers, students, and parents get back to work, because participants in a learning organization recognize that they are on a journey to get better—better as individual and group learners. And— they know they never arrive. This intrinsically rewarding focus provides the motivation to continue pushing toward the future and seeking wisdom. After all, this continuous effort to adapt and evolve makes the school a learning organization.

However, even though many schools are not excellent or even good, the author has yet to come across a school that does not exhibit at least some learning organization characteristics. These attributes can serve as the foundation upon which to build toward excellence. It is time to begin looking at schools as arenas of possibility for experimentation and growth rather than collections of deficits needing fixes.

We hope that one day all schools will be great schools. But any school can begin this journey if the leader or leaders in the school have the courage and central office support to risk the *LTL* practices of open, honest inquiry with the goal of enabling participants to develop their individual and collective empowerment. Greatness is not a product of restoration, repair, or fixing. It is an attribute of innovation, creation, and invention.

One final point needs to be made in this chapter. Today, we have problems that clearly need addressing. Unfortunately, those in positions of political and economic authority in our society seem to lack a belief in or trust in those over whom they can exert power. This, as proposed in this text, has certainly been the case with schools. These folks in authority lack a thinking framework that would allow them to overcome the limited understanding afforded them by the positivist, objectivist paradigm. Their limited thinking comes from a place of knowing, rather than a place of learning.

These folks are trapped and imprisoned by the limits of their thinking. Indeed, we are all caught in this trap. The title of this chapter is "A Different Patriotism." A patriot is someone devoted to her or his country. This means working to secure the best possible future for that country and its citizens. We are reaching the limits of positivism. In order to secure a best future we need a new philosophical paradigm for thinking about our country, our world, and our relationships.

Our technical ability, and the arrogance it produces, is outdistancing our moral and ethical understanding. This is the dilemma we face, the paradox we have created, and the challenge we must address. We cannot continue to define the world as separated objects that we can control. It is time to begin to understand that we don't know what we think we know. We must now begin to think and examine the world together as one that we can influence, for good or for evil. This is learning. This is seeking wisdom.

True leaders are teachers. True teachers are learners. True learners are leaders. True leader, teacher, learners recognize the limits of their knowledge and seek wisdom. The next chapter examines the limits of our knowledge in another way. It questions our concepts related to time. Specifically, it questions the notion of the present. Is the concept "now" part of our technically arrogant frontier thinking that generates false and dangerous assumptions about reality that limit our learning and the pursuit of wisdom?

Chapter Six

Now Is Not Real

The limitations posed by modern positivist thinking in relationship to the complex changes that are occurring in our society and our world were discussed in chapter 5. When we restrict ourselves to looking only through objective eyes our focus is limited to a narrow view that hides opportunities to recognize the existence of a broader reality. Think of it as skinny thinking. The positivist, objective knower is limited to understanding only cause-effect relationships that are a part of but not all of reality.

However, our positivist concepts of the nature of time may contain another limitation. Thinking in terms of the present or "now" may be a concept that interferes with the quality of our knowing. We can recall, read about, and often romanticize the past. More importantly, we can learn from that past, and we hope there is a future that we can imagine and help bring into being. But does the concept of "the present" limit our thinking? Is there really such a time?

Much of the previous paragraph is written in the present tense: a convenient human construct invented to help us understand reality, but it may have a certain automatic quality that restricts thought. We use the concept of "now" whenever we talk about or write something in the present tense. For example, the author can say, "It is raining," because drops of moisture are silently sliding through the air outside his office window. But the odds are that when you read these words, that statement is no longer true. So the presentation of those three words is an abstraction dependent upon your imagination.

Human ability to communicate the abstract meaning each of us has constructed was presented in chapter 3 through a cabin metaphor. Each of us constructs an individual view of reality: a sort of cabin that contains our thinking. Our language provides the windows and doors that enable others to see reflections of those constructions. We look into the windows of others' constructed mind dwellings and sometimes they invite us to come in the door so that we gain a better view.

However, in examining and comparing our thoughts and beliefs with those of others, we need to remember that all of our constructions are images of reality and not actual reality. They are abstractions. Reality is external to the human mind. The problem is that when we are talking in the present, the image becomes flattened. It is a static representation of a dynamic reality. Nothing changes in the present, but in reality, change never stops.

Saying "I am writing this sentence" is not a true statement. You can read the words and construct a meaning from the words. You can conjure up an image of a man writing. But the statement cannot literally be true. Some time ago, the forward-thinking folks at Rowman & Littlefield chose to publish this manuscript. Eventually, advertisements were written for the text. Perhaps you encountered one of them or maybe you obtained the book because a friend recommended it to you. Perhaps you saw the author make a presentation at a conference and were so impressed that you rushed right out of the session and got your copy.

However, if you are reading these words now—correction—if you recently read these words, then all of the events just described will happen in the author's future, but happened at some time in your past. So your image of a man writing the text "now" exists only in your own mind. You must imagine it. The written words provided you with a window into which you looked and constructed a man writing. The writer's ego wants—correction—wanted to know if he was handsome.

WELCOME TO NEVERLAND

Constructivism is both a philosophy and a description of the human process and practice of making meaning. But perhaps our thinking can be trapped by our construction of "now." Most political policy is thought about and written for a constructed sense of the moment: as solutions for *now* problems that are rapidly becoming or likely have already become quandaries of the past. They are not necessarily the difficulties we will face in the future and perhaps they are not real problems at all, but fabricated crises manufactured by our fear of the future.

Therefore, we co-construct now but forget that it is really past now. The problem with the nature of this construct is that it supposedly occupies a place between the past and the future. But the instant it takes us to comprehend what "is happening" keeps moving from the future into the past. The author writing *now* is actually fairly old history. Actually, if this text is any good, you may be reading it long after the author has departed from this Earth. Actually a nice thought, because it gives him certain immortality.

In the not so distant past, the concept of "present" was a convenient and helpful tool for understanding our perceptions. "Now" makes us feel safe. It is a space in which we can figuratively rest and catch our breath, because there is no change in "now." There are only states of being: I am hungry; I am happy; I am in love. But as the rate of change, at least the rate of technological change has accelerated, perhaps our concept of now needs to change, or at least we need to learn to better recognize the limitations of *the present* as a concept.

The present has some utility as a tool for understanding the status of beliefs, emotions, practices, laws, rules, and customs that have been in effect in the recent past; because no one has challenged or changed them, they are likely to be in effect in the near future. We commonly say such things as "I pledge allegiance to the flag of the United States of America," "I hate spinach," "Middle school comes after elementary school," "The speed limit is 70 mph," "Thou shalt not covet thy neighbor's wife," or "We have dessert after dinner." However, the author's grandson rejects this last statement.

The point is that *nowness* has some utility. It gives us a way to describe what seems to be current. Indeed, President Clinton found it useful to say "it depends on what your meaning of the word 'is' is," which earned him the label of "existential Willie" by one commentator (Noah, 1998). The problem is that thinking in terms of now can be a thinking trap that tends to deny the reality of never-ending change.

The limitations of the thinking behind our political policies and practices hold dire consequences for our nation. The conclusion drawn in this text is that we do not know what we think we know. One of the consequences of our perception of the present may lead us to continue making the same mistakes repeatedly. We think in terms of *now* and sense an emergency, causing us to address symptoms of problems rather than underlying causes. The following list provides examples.

- In 2005 we were closely focused on events in the Gulf of Mexico and the destruction of New Orleans by Hurricane Katrina. Seven years later the same levees that were responsible for much of the devastation *are* still in New Orleans and for the most part, unchanged. What can we say we *now know* that changed our practice?
- In 1989, the oil tanker *Exxon Valdez* spilled massive amounts of oil in waters off the Alaska shoreline. What was done to prevent such future catastrophes? What did we learn from that experience? Then in 2010 the Deep Water Horizon oil rig blew up in the Gulf of Mexico, spreading a tremendous volume of oil along the American Coast. What can we say we

now know that changed our practice? Did we learn from our continued efforts to go longer and deeper in pursuit of a finite resource?
- We are continually searching for and expanding our focus on non-renewable resources. Are we sufficiently developing alternative sources of energy, as have other nations? Have we developed effective mass transit systems? Other nations have. Have we made our automobiles significantly smaller and substantially more fuel efficient? Others have, but American television ads still keep us focused on our fascination with big trucks.
- Four decades ago, we were engaged in a war in Vietnam. We lost that war. Prior to our engagement the French were at war there. They lost that war. We have been at war in Afghanistan for over ten years and have only recently withdrawn from our concurrent war in Iraq, although we still have many people from the private sector engaged there. What have we learned about the nature of guerilla warfare during the past fifty years?
- Two decades ago, the Soviet Union was engaged in a war in Afghanistan, fighting the same people we are fighting today. They lost that war and withdrew after a nine-year engagement. What can we say we *now know* about the nature of guerilla war and political involvement that has changed our policies and practices?
- In 1929, the American stock market crashed generating a very severe worldwide depression. That event, known as the "Great Depression," was the product of over-speculation by financial experts. Beginning in late 2007, we experienced the "Great Recession" due to over-speculation by financial experts. What did we know in 2007 that demonstrated what we had learned about over speculation in the seventy-eight years since the Great Depression?
- We have had numerous periods of recession between these two events. What have we learned from each of these events that will help prevent future recessions and depressions? Why did we not know these things when each of those recessionary periods was *now*? Why are we not applying some of the lessons learned *now*?

These events and many others have captured our attention in the moment. But each of those moments was replaced by other *now* events. A way we might avoid repeating some of these failures of knowing is to begin thinking beyond our sense of now. What if we had looked at the past to help guide our future actions rather than focusing entirely on immediate events? If we had done so, we might have built stronger levees in New Orleans or have done so after Katrina.

We might have developed alternative energy sources that would substantially reduce our dependence on oil. President Jimmy Carter advocated such an effort in what came to be called his "malaise speech." It seems that Americans wanted to stay in *now* back then and President Carter did not get reelected. But had we addressed the energy issue, we would have been less dependent upon Middle Eastern oil. Perhaps we would have avoided engaging in two simultaneous Middle Eastern guerilla wars, creating much of the massive debt that seems to be stalling our recovery from the recession caused by our failure to learn from previous periods of financial over speculation.

We still seem stuck in *now* and focusing on the present. As a result, we fail to retain the lessons of the past and apply them to our future. Our goals are identified in terms of an assumed present state—a positivist trap that fails to see beyond that which is immediate, settling for an understanding of the complicated parts in the present, but ignoring the complex relationships that existed in the real world of the past and will likely contribute to future events. This is a trap based upon the assumption of knowing that creates a sense of urgency soon forgotten. It avoids seeking wisdom.

Chapter 3 outlined the development of the modern positivist thinking framework and how it came about in response to the limitations of a dependence upon magic, sorcery, and myth as sources of knowledge. Is it possible that thinking in *now* is part of a modern positivist thinking trap that creates a new magic and a new sorcery practiced by learned people who create new myths that blind them to reality because they do not recognize that the limits of their knowledge are dictated by seeing reality as narrow cause-effect relationships, restricted even more by what seems to be happening *now*?

Are we suffering from both tunnel vision and nearsightedness? Could it be that by thinking in a state of *now* we are blind to our own ignorance? Does our technical arrogance lead us to a false security in the absolute power of our complicated mechanical knowledge? Do we fail to follow Sternberg's (2004) suggestion to seek wisdom that looks to the past and the future? Do we assume that our *now* is real and get stuck in the mire of complication that it represents: a sort of Peter Pan syndrome for adults? Welcome to Neverland USA!

Perhaps a better way to think is to remember that the present is a tool that has some utility for helping us to create images to share what exists in our minds and is a product of our ability to use language, but that reality involves the past we have lived as individuals and indirectly experienced as members of the human species, and it serves as the only guide that can help us influence the development of a better future. Perhaps we can seek wisdom, attempting to understand that there is a past from which we may draw guidance as we search for truth in a future that will reveal more than we know.

THROWING OUT THE BABY WITH THE BATH WATER

Each of these failures to recall lessons of the past as we look at the future have had very important implications for our country and its people. However, we can find perhaps the most significant implications we will experience in the way we educate our young. Chapter 4 described how our focus on schooling has been *narrow*. The emphasis on fixing schools is also trapped by *now* thinking. These *narrow* and *now*, modern positivist thinking structures are generating serious risks for our young. And quite frankly, the young really are our future.

An ideal example of this adult Peter Pan syndrome has been our government's response to recent international test scores comparing American students to students from other countries. This is a pernicious and dangerously misleading modern *fact* that just won't go away. These test comparisons demonstrate that overall American test scores are mediocre, but these test score results are facts that disguise the reality of both the excellence of many of our schools and the range in education quality delivered to students across the nation. Let's examine these facts in a context that extends beyond *now*.

The conclusion drawn when *A Nation at Risk* (National Commission on Excellence in Education, 1983) was first published was that our schools were falling behind due to a rising tide of mediocrity and creating an emergency that must be immediately addressed: a *now* response. *Program for International Student Assessment* (PISA, 2009) results were released in December 2010. This international standardized test comparison indicated that American students are only obtaining "average" scores: results quite similar to those of the past.

The *now* response from education policy makers was to declare an emergency that must be immediately addressed: the same response generated by the Reagan White House nearly thirty years ago. In a speech, Secretary of Education Arne Duncan (2010) made the following comments about these results.

- Here in the United States, we have looked forward eagerly to the 2009 PISA results. But the findings, I'm sorry to report, show that the United States needs to urgently accelerate student learning to remain competitive in the knowledge economy of the 21st century. (p. 3)
- President Obama has repeatedly warned that the nation that "out-educates us today will out-compete us tomorrow. And the PISA results, to be brutally honest, show that a host of developed nations are out-educating us." (p. 7)

- Finland, Korea, and Canada are consistent high-performers. And the jewel of China's education system, Shanghai, debuted this year as the highest scoring participant globally. (p. 8)
- The hard truth is that other high-performing nations have passed us by during the last two decades. (p. 10)
- Americans need to wake up to this educational reality—instead of napping at the wheel while emerging competitors prepare their students for economic leadership. (p. 11)
- So the big picture from PISA is one of educational stagnation, at a time of fast-rising demand for highly-educated workers. The mediocre performance of America's students is a problem we cannot afford to accept and cannot afford to ignore. (p. 19)

But is it true, as Secretary Duncan suggested, that these nations are out-educating us and that they have passed us by?

One of the perennial high-scoring countries is Singapore. Chapter 4 examined Yong Zhao's (2010) analysis of standardized exams focused on Chinese cities and states. He concluded that their emphasis on testing came about because of the centuries-old cultural focus on tests. Paul Houston (2007) reported on an interview by Fareed Zakaria of Singapore's Minister of Education. Zakaria asked why Singapore's students scored so much higher but did not do as well as the Americans ten to twelve years after the test. The minister said that their society has a focus on deciding the merits of an individual based upon a test, but that America's meritocracy was based upon talent.

The highest scores on the latest PISA tests went to another Chinese city. Shanghai has always been the crown of national Chinese education. Jiang Xueqin is deputy principal of Peking University High School, and director of its international division. He discussed these results in an editorial appearing in the *Wall Street Journal* (Jiang, 2010). He said that Shanghai's scores are actually a sign of the problem in China's schools.

Jiang explained that the emphasis on testing enables Chinese students to develop excellent skills for service as mid-level accountants, computer programmers, and technocrats that are needed in a socialist society, but not the innate inquisitiveness and imagination, and moral/ethical responsibilities needed for higher education and the knowledge economy. Indeed, he said they must send their students abroad to develop those attributes.

Could it be that the ongoing effort in the United States to define school success as efficient delivery of curriculum in the small realm of tested standards rather than developing the imagination and creativity that have always been the hallmark of American ingenuity may actually lead to throwing out the baby with the bath water? Singapore was the highest scorer on the previous PISA tests and their scores continue to be among the highest. Let's compare what Secretary Duncan had to say with a recent statement from Prime Minister Lee of Singapore regarding the 2009 PISA results. Minister Lee said

> I think we should do more to nurture the whole child. . . . Every child is different, every child has his own interests, his own academic inclinations and aptitudes and our aim should be to provide him with a good education that suits him, one which enables him to achieve his potential and build on his strengths and talents. (Slade, 2010)

Minister Lee's statement stands in stark contrast to our focus on standards and testing. His statement was focused on attempting to develop the creative potential of Chinese students. He is correct. IBM Corporation recently completed a study of 1500 chief executive officers from sixty countries and thirty industries. They found that successfully navigating an increasingly complex business world will require very creative employees.

Specifically, the IBM study found that they need individuals who can make more business model changes, invite disruptive innovation, create new ways to innovate, are comfortable with ambiguity, and are able to alter the status quo and invent new business models (IBM Global CEO Study, 2010). Anyone who has observed changes in the business world within the past several years could make similar predictions. But just what is creativity and are we preparing our children for this increasingly complex world with our focus on standards and testing?

Creativity is required for discovering and inventing new ideas and knowledge. It is focused on questions such as what can or could be and what do I or we want? It is not about fixing a problem or discovering a single right answer. In fact, the idea of problem solving, that is, getting the right answer, which is the basic requirement on standardized tests, actually hinders creativity.

How are we doing at developing the creativity of young people? An article in *Newsweek* reported ongoing research started in 1958 analyzing the creativity of American children (Bronson and Merryman, 2010). This research suggested that creativity is a more important factor in the success of children than intelligence. The article reported that Americans were becoming more creative until about 1990. Since that time we have had a slow but steady decline.

Our standards-based curriculum and intense focus on standardized tests may not be responsible for this decline in creativity, although standards were introduced at about the same time that the decline began. It is likely that other factors such as time spent watching television or playing video games play a part. However, our focus on narrowing instruction to testable standards and isolating content areas from one another are certainly not helping our children become more creative or more interested in what school has to offer.

Secretary Duncan also commented that scores of students in Finland were perennially high. Was it because the Finns are focused on mechanically developing educational efficiency by depending on standardized tests that tend to lead schools to focus instruction upon limited curricular areas (math, science, and reading) because they assume that doing so will make their students economically competitive in the job market? Timo Lankinen, Director-General, Finnish National Board of Education, said that their schools were not actually talking a lot about numeracy or literacy (Slade, 2010).

Instead, the Finnish agenda for change is more about twenty-first-century skills that they refer to as "citizen skills." They focus on small class size, greater individualized student attention, increasing experiential learning, and "enabling teachers and students to flourish." The minister concluded that their system would be great when every student and stakeholder says, "I love school" (Slade, 2010).

So educators in Finland are emphasizing early childhood play, individualization, experiential learning, and loving school. These were the practices that were very much in vogue in the touchy-feely, hands-on, self-esteem affirming, open classrooms of the 1970s and 1980s in the United States, and remember, that was just prior to the explosion of new knowledge, invention, and technology that generated the economic successes of the 1980s and 1990s.

Oh, but that was not *now*. So it was forgotten. Historian Diane Ravitch, who until recently was an advocate for standards and NCLB, clearly understands why Finnish schools have been so successful. She said, "Finland seems to be the educational utopia that was envisioned by John Dewey but came to fruition in Finland. Here is a nation that avoids standardized tests altogether, that prizes teacher autonomy, and that has regularly achieved great academic success on PISA" (Ravitch, 2011).

In defense of Secretary Duncan, please note that he correctly acknowledged the high status of teachers in these top-scoring countries and the strong support they receive in their schools and communities. Recognizing the value of teachers in the improvement of schooling is essential. Unlike politicians in the United States who engage in disempowering and overregulating educators, the Canadians credit their school improvement upon their work to improve the status and professionalism of teachers.

Ontario, Canada's Premier Dalton McGuinty discussed their work to build positive working relationships with teachers. He said, "We have worked hard to build a positive, working relationship with our teachers. We do not engage in inflammatory rhetoric. We do not use our teachers as a political punching bag. Public bickering undermines public confidence." McGuinty added that policy development and implementation happen in dialogue with educators. He referenced his mother's advice on his wedding day. She said, "Whatever happens, keep talking. So we keep talking to our teachers" (Slade, 2010).

Unlike American policy makers, our Canadian neighbors are listening to their teachers rather than blaming them for education failure. However, our modern, positivist, *narrow-now* focus has identified lazy teachers and their unions as the culprits behind a perceived mediocre education system that is allowing others to "out-educate us." Obviously Wisconsin's Scott Walker and several other Republican governors around the nation who have focused on ending conversations with teachers' union representatives and Canada's Premier McGuinty have very different views of the value of talking.

What Secretary Duncan doesn't report and perhaps doesn't know is that U.S. scores in schools with 10 percent or lower poverty rates actually received higher scores than schools in Finland where the poverty rate is only 4 percent (Ravitch, 2011; Tirozzi, 2011). Could it be that Finland's high scores are related to their low poverty levels? Could poverty actually be the culprit dragging down U.S. test scores and not lazy teachers?

Quality Counts, sponsored by Education Week, is an annual analysis grading the quality of education provided in the fifty states and the District of Columbia (Hightower, 2011). This report annually examines eighteen categories of indicators on a state-by-state basis, including current student achievement, improvements over time, and poverty-based disparities. Unfortunately, the United States as a nation received a D-plus grade for our overall efforts to improve education. Massachusetts had the highest rating: a "B." Sadly, Louisiana, Mississippi, New Mexico, and West Virginia all received grades of "F."

A truly enlightening aspect of this report was a category entitled "Chance for Success," which contains thirteen subcategories. Particularly interesting were three of the subcategories in that section: the state-by-state comparisons of the percentages of students who scored proficient or better on National Assessment of Educational Progress in fourth-grade reading, eighth-grade math, and family income.

The family income variable, for this report, was the percentage of children living in families with incomes at least 200 percent above the poverty rate of $22,050 for a family of four. Therefore, a family of four would be at the 200 percent rate with a family income of $44,100, which is still rather low. Table 6.1 compares the five highest income states and the five lowest income states, and shows the mean score for each group.

This is a most revealing part of the Quality Counts report. The five states with the highest percentage of family incomes above 200 percent of the poverty rate have about twice as many students achieving proficiency or better in fourth-grade reading (47.9 percent) and eighth-grade math (43.9

Table 6.1. NAEP Scores of Five States Ranking Highest and Five States Ranking Lowest in Family Income

	Family Income [a]	4th Grade Reading [b]	8th Grade Math [b]
Five Highest Ranking			
Massachusetts	72.7	78.4	51.7
Connecticut	73.6	78.4	39.8
New Jersey	71	78.4	44.4
Maryland	72.4	78.4	41.1
High Mean	*72.8*	*78.4*	*43.9*
Five Lowest Ranking			
Texas	51.1	27.7	36.2
District of Columbia	50.7	16.8	11.2
New Mexico	48.1	19.8	24.8
Arkansas	47.1	21.7	15.2
Mississippi	45.5	21.7	15.2
Low Mean	*48.5*	*22.7*	*22.9*

Source: Hightower (2011).
[a] percentages of children's families with income at least double the poverty rate
[b] percentage of students scoring proficient or above

percent) than the five states with the lowest family income (22.7 percent in fourth-grade reading and 22.9 percent in eighth-grade math).

Ravitch (2011) addressed this shameful and growing poverty rate. She noted that Isabel Sawhill of the Brookings Institution reported that more than 20 percent of American children live in poverty and expects that number to reach 25 percent by 2014. Earlier in the text, the question regarding whether our schools or our society have been failing our children was raised. The evidence is clear. It is not that our schools have failed. It is that our market system has failed for a large percentage of our population.

The greatest obstacle for student learning and school success is poverty. But policy makers and media blame schools. Our *narrow, now* positivist thinking limits our view to market values and applies coin-operation market norms to the social institutions that bind us together. We are endangering our future because we are failing so many of our children. We have made ourselves accountable to our market system rather than holding our market system responsible for improving our nation and its citizens. We seem to be very busy throwing out the baby with the bath water.

BLINDED BY OUR ASSUMPTIONS

Why have we developed such a *narrow* and *now* focus? The emergence of the modern positivist paradigm that generated our reliance on the idea of the inviolability of scientific objectivity has been discussed at length. The problem is not that an examination of objective relationships is bad. Indeed, objectivity is an essential element for analyzing facts, testing reality, and examining the relative value of contemplated change.

The problem is that we assume that a relationship described objectively is a total relationship, and it is not. We fail to inquire more deeply. The comparison of family income and NAEP scores presented above is purely objective. It raises questions about the conclusion that American education is mediocre, simply by adding one additional variable to the discussion. The variable added is poverty. The comparison questioned a conclusion based upon PISA test scores, a complicated data set, by adding a variable that gave the discussion greater complexity and made it a better reflection of reality.

David Bohm (1996) was a quantum scientist who left his work as a physicist to examine the complex nature of human communication and thinking processes. Reading his work led the author to explore the ideas of others Bohm had inspired and to an interest in experimenting with inquiry. Bohm concluded that the outcome or product of human thought was belief and that each individual's beliefs are his or her core assumptions.

Bohm theorized that we fail to recognize that all relationships are limited by the recognition ability of the observer and that all observers have limited recognition ability. Therefore, our thoughts, which are products derived from an examination of events colored by our assumptions, are always limited, or as evolutionary biologist David Sloan Wilson (2008) succinctly observed, "deception begins with perception" (p. 282).

America became a country during the time of the emergence of the modern scientific paradigm. As a nation, we found great success in the application of scientific thinking regarding economics. Indeed, Adam Smith's *The Wealth of Nations* (Smith, republished 2009) was first published in 1776 and served as the philosophical foundation for the Industrial Revolution. This foundation rests on the assumptions that free-market economies are more productive and therefore of great benefit to their societies, because humans are rational.

Consequently, we have built much of American society around a free-market theme. Economics is the study of scarcity, and market economies are based upon human beings' collective decisions about the values of goods and services, and on how difficult those items are to acquire. In other words, market economies work, and work very efficiently because they are determined by rational analysis. Contemporary education thinking is dominated by market-based ideas grounded in modern positivist economics. These ideas include merit pay, charter schools, and using value-added test results in making high-stakes decisions.

Florida's governor, Rick Scott, and former D.C. public schools chief Michelle Rhee recently announced their "Students First" partnership (*Gov. Rick Scott, Michelle Rhee Announce Partnership*, 2011). They believe they can improve schools and teacher quality by increasing accountability measures and by giving parents and students more options. Their plan includes school vouchers for low-income students and merit pay plans for teachers. Scott said, "If we create competition, everybody will improve. We see it in the business world and the same thing will happen in education" (*Gov. Rick Scott, Michelle Rhee Announce Partnership*, 2011).

Certainly Scott, Rhee, and many others sincerely believe that competition will improve schools. But this belief is an assumption. Yes, in the United States it is a powerful assumption. It is based on Adam Smith's 235-year-old notion that humans are rational and that we apply our rationality in all of our decisions. But the work of Dan Ariely (2009) and others clearly demonstrates that this is not so.

Indeed, if you will watch television advertisements for just a few minutes you will realize that just as Ariely has found, we humans are irrational. Those ads focus upon addressing our social needs and not our market needs. Why else would someone spend thousands of extra dollars to purchase a Cadillac rather than an equally equipped Chevrolet? Both are made by the same company and offer about the same level of comfort. But the Cadillac gives you a higher status. Yes, our rationality is one of those *facts* that we are discovering is really a *myth*. It may actually be *factitious*: a word that means produced by humans rather than by natural forces.

RACE TO THE TOP: NO RACE, NO TOP

One of the *now* events closer to home for the author is the state of Tennessee's award of the $500 million U.S. Department of Education's *Race to the Top* grant (*First to the Top*, 2010). This is especially important because the author's grandson attends public school in Tennessee. The Tennessee *First to the Top* website describes the grant as an unprecedented federal investment designed to reward states leading the way in comprehensive, coherent, statewide education reform.

Some of the core elements of this grant call for Tennessee schools to adopt national common core standards, enhance data collection and assessment systems, develop a teacher and principal evaluation process linked to standardized test results with 35 percent based upon Tennessee's value added system, and anticipate that up to "10 percent of teachers may be classified as ineffective and removed" (*First to the Top*: Executive Summary, 2010). Anticipating that a teacher shortfall may occur as a result, the state is enhancing alternative teacher licensure development, as well as efforts to encourage charter schools.

It is quite ironic that almost immediately after the state of Tennessee announced receipt of the *First to the Top* award, a study by Nashville's own Vanderbilt University and the RAND Corporation found that providing teachers with test-based bonus incentives does not increase student test scores (Moran, 2010). By the way, this was a three-year study that took place in the public schools of Nashville, which is also the state capital. Clearly, those who participated in the development of *First to the Top* made irrational decisions using market-based assumptions about the nature of teacher motivation that are not supported by objective fact.

Unfortunately, these market-inspired plans, representative of the same mechanistic thinking that inspired *No Child Left Behind* (2001), are based upon assumptions that will not play out as anticipated. They are expressions of our modern, positivist, wisdom-limiting paradigm that traps us into thinking "now," so that we are unable to see the hidden complex relationships presented by the realities of the past and the possibilities of the future.

We do not look to see beyond the myriad complicated parts that block our view of reality. We assume the parts that we see in our immediate view are all there is to see. We assume that large numbers of curriculum standards assessed by standardized tests that can only assess lower-level thinking and learning skills in a limited number of curriculum categories truly reflect what our students need to know to meet their needs in a future that we have not really thought about.

We assume that students fail to get high scores because their teachers are ineffective. We assume that any persons who demonstrate competence in a subject area, as defined by a test score, will be good teachers, and find a fast track to get those folks into the classroom. We assume that because many students in some schools are not doing well, then all schools must be failing. We assume that teachers are ineffective because they are lazy. We assume that we can overcome this laziness by providing them with market-inspired incentives or potential punishments.

We seem blinded to the depth of disadvantage that poverty creates for learners and have been increasing the numbers of children living in poverty for several years. We are blind to the success of many of our former students who have finished school and lead the development of innovation and technology around the globe. We are blind to the feedback we get from around the world related to what has worked and what has not worked in other places.

We assume that market-driven efficiencies will deliver the quality education that our young people need. We assume that the high test scores of some other nations are a reflection of our mediocrity and attempt to *fix* ourselves to be more like them, but are blind to their efforts to be more like us. We are trapped by our assumptions in an endless Neverland cycle of narrowness and nowness.

We are ruled by volumes of factitious statements that reflect our narrow and now thinking. We are attempting to fix our schools as if they are factory production lines. We are treating our children as if they were the widgets the factory line produces. We ignore the successful qualities demonstrated by the teachers and students in many schools. We assume that our fears are reality, and we are blind to our own success.

What does this mean for our future? The impact of our focus on curriculum standards, our increased dependence on high-stakes tests, our increased emphasis on creating efficient instructional delivery systems regardless of whether the instruction provided is appropriate to the learning capabilities or the learning needs of children, and a focus on attempting to improve instruction by connecting teacher pay to those assessments will fail. The result will be the opposite of what Secretary Duncan, President Obama, and our elected representatives from both major parties at the national and state levels hope to achieve.

Our schools are being used as an excuse for failures in other areas. Ravitch (2011) discussed the high PISA scores in Finland and the even higher scores in Shanghai. She noted that both countries have improved their schools by strengthening their public sectors and providing strong support for public schools rather than deregulating and supporting private schools. The Canadians are doing the same. For the past thirty years, America seems to be stuck, unable to recognize what valuable assets our schools have been to our society and should be in the future.

Can we overcome the traps of narrow objective analysis and the limits of thinking in now that feed fear of the future? Can we escape from Neverland? Market-driven changes will not generate improvements in a system that needs to be governed by social norms. The author's grandchild needs a teacher who sees him as a whole and important human being and not as a test score that will either reduce or improve her bottom line.

Contemporary narrow, now education policy mechanisms represent a near total acceptance of the value of market norms over social norms and a focus on trying to create an accountable educational system. In so doing, we will sacrifice the practice of responsibility that has been characteristic of the best in American schooling and the best of American citizenship.

A focus on developing the quality of responsibility in schooling is the direction in which other countries have elected to move. It seems they are capable of seeking wisdom and moving away from the *narrow-now* thinking that traps us. Let's hope we will be able to realize the limits we are placing on our collective future before our modern, wisdom-limiting, market-driven policies completely sabotage our schools and deprive our children of the quality future they might achieve.

CAN WE FOCUS ON THE FUTURE?

What would education policies be like if we did have more of a future focus? Would we create a single set of standards that focus a very large, overlapping, and growing range of knowledge, skills, and attributes into isolated subject areas and assess students' learning with tests that can only measure lower-level skills? Or could education policies address the need to look at the complexity of human needs and motivation, and help inspire our young to develop the best possible futures?

Would we recognize that we need our young to develop a deep understanding of the relationships between and among curricular areas and develop their abilities to challenge current knowledge and create new knowledge? Would it be some combination of skill sets extended into a variety of possible options and explorations that enlist individual student interest in the mix? Or will we continue to limit their futures by trying to capture and keep an imagined present that we claim to *know*? Could we

- Work to overcome outdated elements of an organizational structure originally modeled after the Industrial Age factory of the nineteenth and twentieth centuries and designed to efficiently transform generations of immigrants from foreign countries and the rural areas of the nation into factory workers?
- Begin to question and challenge a political system that distrusts educators and employs political practices and policies that disempower educational practitioners' ability to accomplish the very changes demanded by those who control the system?
- Realize that overcoming poverty, the enormous new challenge assigned to our schools, has never been attempted before and understand that this incredibly worthwhile goal will require a great deal of cost and experimentation by educators?
- Focus upon developing students' creativity, initiative, effort, and judgment—the attributes they most need for success today and will likely need in the future?
- Develop school and community cultures that support learning and risk taking?

- Recognize and build upon the strategies of responsible practice that good teachers have always brought to the profession rather than attempting to replace these natural human, social norm-based qualities with market accountability tactics?

Will we learn to seek wisdom and recognize the paradox that accepting our limited knowledge of reality allows us to begin to realize our unlimited potential? Or will we settle for the narrow Neverland of now? Peter Senge (1990) identified inability to see the forest for the trees as an organizational learning disability. He recognized the limits of complicated mechanical thinking that lead us to become overwhelmed with complication and fail to recognize the complex relationships presented just beyond.

We must learn to challenge the complications that restrict our view and seek to understand the complex multilayered nature of reality. We must understand our ignorance so that we may accept our limited knowledge. As Parker Palmer said (2004), we must live the questions. Inquiry, a set of practices that enable us to challenge our knowledge limits and pursue wisdom, is the subject of the next chapter.

Chapter Seven

Seek Wisdom: Lead Inquiry

Few of us know how to talk to one another in productive ways. That is, talk to one another in ways that get to the deep cultural and structural issues that divide us. Most of us are unable to talk to one another so that we realize and challenge our own and other's assumptions about what is real and what is true and extend our thinking beyond the limits imposed by modern positivist, narrow, now thinking.

We don't know how to talk to one another in ways that enable us to co-create a better future together. In schools and in society, we have great difficulty in overcoming the obstacles that interfere with efforts to improve learning and understanding for students and adults. However, as argued in chapter 5, our schools do a better job in having the conversations that address these barriers than do most other organizations.

Learning about and practicing inquiry based upon honest dialogue and productive discussion provides the wisdom-seeking framework that individuals and groups need to generate the productive conversations that will enable them to address the divisions within our society, to effectively investigate learning needs, and to develop, modify, and/or make practical application of school improvement strategies that have been adopted by schools and districts. Inquiry is the action process in the *LTL* triad.

Inquiry in this chapter is presented as a framework for improving the work of educators, but similar frameworks are commonly advocated for use in business, social organizations, and even political organizations (Brown, 2005; Ellinor and Gerard, 1998; Isaacs, 1999a, 1999b; Palmer, 2004; Senge, 1990; Vella, 1995). It is best to think about this inquiry framework as a continuum that extends from *open inquiry* to *focused inquiry*. Open inquiry is a process for developing healthy organizational culture. Focused inquiry provides the actionable steps, plans, and strategies that participants in the organization can take for improving their work.

Open inquiry seeks to discover the unique and individual voice of each of the organization's participants. From the authentic voices of individuals, a collective voice surfaces that recognizes and values the unique contributions each participant makes to the group. Out of this process, foci emerge from the recognition of the shared interests and individual attributes of the participants. Then, group members become engaged in focusing inquiry upon the specific issues, concerns, and problems they perceive. In other words, open inquirers uncover who and what the group is and focused inquirers decide what the group should do.

VOICE, CULTURE, MISSION, AND VISION

Sergiovanni (2008) suggested that our schools need to become "tight on values and loose on how values are embodied in the practices of teaching, supervision, and administration" (p. 77). This means that leadership work is cultural work. The educational leader's job is the development of a shared culture: a close but not absolute agreement by participants, on the values of educational practice.

It doesn't mean that school leaders shouldn't focus on traditional management functions. Such functions are critical and a prerequisite for any school improvement. Schools must have the supplies, materials, and efficient schedules in place for teaching and learning to occur. But much more is needed for effective schooling. School leaders must do more than manage. The goal of management is to enable *LTL* processes among the children and the adults within the school. Principals must manage and lead. More accurately, they must manage to lead. The work of the principal and other school leaders is to manage so that learning occurs and improves.

This is the leader's teaching umbrella. The goal of efficient management becomes the creation of opportunities for change so that teachers, students, and others in the school are free from as much bureaucratic/structural control as possible; this control must be replaced with opportunities for developing individual responsibility and shared purpose. The term responsibility rather that ownership, buy-in, or accountability is used purposefully here.

Buy-in is a term referring to the trades. We buy goods and services, but should not buy our ideas and beliefs; we should develop them. They should come from within, rather than from someone else's shelf. Accountability is a power term. A person is accountable to someone who has power over that individual, regardless of his or her beliefs. However, a responsible person is conscientious and dependable regardless of the power that another may exercise. All true professionals and authentically ethical individuals are responsible people. Their actions are based upon the responsibilities they feel for others and not because they are accountable to others.

So, how can principals and other school leaders reduce bureaucratic/structural control and help teachers, students, and others acquire responsibility for their learning and actions? They need to become students and teachers of communication and generate the conversations that help teachers and others discover, examine, and surface their individual voices: their tacit beliefs, their deep and often hidden values, and how these are reflected in their teaching. Then, they must help teachers shape their individual voices into a unified *voice*. This voice will be the mission and vision to which the community of teachers is truly committed.

WHO SPEAKS? WHO LISTENS?

Leaders in schools and in other organizations know that their work is about communicating. All leaders must make communication decisions about who needs to know, what they need to know, when they need to know it, and where and how to tell them. Certainly, the most common reason for speaking is to transmit information. The most common reason for listening is to receive information.

Generally, this communication format is designed to enable participants to understand the rules, expectations, and knowledge transmitted by someone in a position of authority to whom the participants are accountable: students listening to a teacher speaking, teachers listening to a principal speaking. Such speaking and listening are essential for the efficient management of the organization. Without such direct communication an organization (the classroom or the school) would soon be in chaos. However, these essential directive communications limit participant responses, making it difficult for an organization to change in significant ways.

The second type of speaking and listening common in organizations is nonproductive discussion. Participants in these conversations focus on winning the discussion by out-selling or out-arguing other speakers. Listening becomes a tactical search for flaws in other speakers' arguments. Isaacs (1999b) labeled such discussion as "unproductive defensiveness" (p. 41).

We have all been in discussions where some participants engage in debate while most others disengage from the conversation. Active participants focus upon winning rather than understanding alternatives and developing options that could lead to a viable solution for all participants. Virtually every principal, every teacher, and many parents have been in faculty meetings, team meetings, committee meetings, IEP meetings, and other meetings where participants are unable to reach agreement.

Generally, these meetings end in an argument, a mandated solution, or both. Such solution limits are exacerbated when there is a power differential between participants, such as between principal and teachers. Decisions reached usually reflect the views of the leader/manager rather than a view supported by all or even most participants. In these situations, whether they know it or not, those with organizational authority depend upon the compliance of accountable subordinates rather than the commitment of responsible agents, to a plan of action.

INQUIRY SKILLS: DIALOGUE AND DISCUSSION

Fortunately there are two additional forms of conversation that can help schools challenge the modern, objectively framed conversation that limits participants to the directive-receptive communications needed for organizational maintenance but minimizes change. They also get beyond the divisiveness of nonproductive discussions that allows for no change at all. These forms are *open dialogue* and *productive discussion*. Successful dialogue and discussion depend upon four tools that are simple to understand but difficult to practice. These tools are *deep listening, respecting, suspending assumptions*, and *voicing* (Isaacs, 1999a; 1999b).

Deep listening requires that conversation participants follow other participants' thinking so that the listener begins to blend with someone and to participate fully in understanding how the speaker understands. This means *respecting* others as legitimate so that one can listen to the sense in what they are saying. Participants must also *suspend* their *assumptions* and the certainty about their opinions by not judging others.

Isaacs also refers to balancing advocacy with inquiry by taking a balcony view, allowing all voices to be heard and all views presented. Each participant becomes a keen observer of all participants in the conversation including herself or himself. *Voicing* is the fourth tool. It means speaking personal truths to show our genuine selves by talking from the heart and mind, as we recognize that there are multiple truths: what is true for one individual may not be true for another. Each participant must find a balance between her or his voice and those of others.

The use of these tools in dialogue enables participants to

1. See the whole among the parts.
2. See the relationships among the parts.
3. Learn through inquiry and disclosure.

4. Create [a] shared meaning among many. (Ellinor and Gerard, 1998).

Dialogue allows participants in a conversation to be open with one another and explore hidden possibilities. In dialogue a democracy of ideas occurs because all participants learn to listen with respect to all other participants and suspend their assumptions about the ideas of others. Therefore, the ideas of each participant gain an equal hearing within the minds of other participants.

On the other hand, discussion depends on the tools of listening, respecting, suspending opinions, and voicing so that participants in a conversation are able to

1. Break issues and problems into their component parts
2. Make distinctions between the parts visible to participants
3. Justify or defend assumptions
4. Persuade, tell, and sell
5. Gain agreement on one meaning. (Ellinor and Gerard, 1998)

Of course, justifying positions, defending assumptions, and attempting to persuade are common in nonproductive discussion. However, the purpose of nonproductive discussion is to win a conversation by getting others to give in. An agreement gained in nonproductive discussion reflects the will of one or a few members of the group. The execution of such an agreement is based upon compliance, which is strictly a function of management. Productive discussion deemphasizes justifying, defending, and selling. It focuses on understanding issues and problems by examining the parts and working to gain agreement or reach a solution.

Together, open dialogue and productive discussion create the path that enables a group to move toward wisdom. Productive discussion is necessary for groups to reach consensus or to develop a plan of action. However, discussion without dialogue greatly limits participants' knowledge and understanding of the perspectives and possibilities that can be presented by other participants.

This shared knowledge is necessary for truly understanding an issue. It is knowledge required for seeking wisdom and is essential for leading change. Dialogue is a process for group discovery, inclusion, and acceptance. It is a step toward seeking wisdom because it breaks the bounds of knowledge to reveal possibilities. Without dialogue, participants don't know the views of others, often don't even consider that perceptions might be different, or that considering others' outlooks could have value. Dialogue allows individuals to walk in others' shoes, creating a broader frame of reference and understanding.

Productive discussion is a process for developing shared commitment. Participants are able to freely examine all of the possibilities, risks, and fears that have surfaced in dialogue. All participants jointly own these possibilities, risks, and fears. Group members are tough on issues but gentle with one another. Effective groups continuously rotate between dialogue and productive discussion in an ongoing, evolving process of discovery and examination. Group members are continually developing a commitment to a shared view: an evolving mission and vision. Consequently, such agreements are self-sustaining and self-renewing.

However, when there is a power differential between participants, the leader has an important responsibility. She or he must create a place in time and space where open dialogue and productive discussion are safe. This is done in two ways. First, a leader must create a communication space by dedicating meetings to inquiry and introduce participants to Isaacs's (1999a; 1999b) four practices or a similar set of ground rules.

Second, in these meetings the leader must restrict her or his own voice and focus on listening, respecting, and suspending assumptions until participants see the leader as an equal participant in the conversation. This is difficult. The leader can facilitate the meetings and restrict her or his voice by expressing no opinions and asking open, honest questions—and only open, honest questions.

Open, honest questions are questions for which the leader does not have an answer. Palmer (2004) described a "dishonest question" or a closed question as one in which the person asking the question assumes that he or she knows what the answer should be (p. 132). It is actually advice, posed as a question. Posing an opinion as a question is a manipulative tactic. Yes, it is a reflection of modern positivist objectively framed thinking: I, the speaker, know what you, the listener, need.

Open, honest questions are not "advice in disguise" (Palmer, 2004, p. 132). This takes practice. As teachers and leaders we are well versed in asking questions designed to achieve a specific answer. This is useful for sharing information in direct instruction. But the moment a leader expresses an opinion, either clearly stated or hidden in a question, dialogue and productive discussion end. Participants hear the leader's opinion as a decision and believe there is little point in continued conversation.

Please note, the suggestion is not that stating opinions or lecturing as a teaching strategy is wrong. Often, the efficiency gained by presenting information in a lecture format is the best possible use of time. However, such pontification is wrong when used as a device for controlling conversational processes and outcomes. Telling is useful for presenting a decision, explaining a process, or giving instructions. It is not useful for engaging a group in decision making, and when used in this way sabotages the leader's effort by generating distrust among participants.

CREATING AN INQUIRY PRACTICE

How can a principal or other school leader generate the practice of open inquiry in a school setting? There is not a specific recipe for generating dialogue and productive discussion. The author's experiences in developing a culture of inquiry in school were described in chapter 2. It is complex and difficult work, but it is the valuable and ultimately rewarding work a wisdom-seeking leader must perform to enhance the operation of the *LTL* triad. After all, the leading, teaching, and learning process is the primary work of the organization.

Inquiry will evolve somewhat differently in each situation. This is because every group and every situation is different. People, places, issues, resources, and beliefs will reveal unique subjects and issues, but inquiry can bring them together in ways that honor these differences yet create unified understanding, purpose, and action. The key is for the leader, especially a principal, to develop a high level of trust and an earnest interest in discovering participant views and helping participants develop their individual voices and collectively generate a unified voice.

Remember, the unified voice that teachers and other participants develop becomes the real mission of the school: the mission for which teachers and principal share responsibility and not just accountability. This voice is the powerful mission for which participants are committed to work and frees the leader from attempting to force compliance for someone else's rules and regulations. Indeed, the development of this voice/mission can extend to students, parents, and the community.

The following suggestions are offered to help start an inquiry process in a school. These ideas are easily adaptable to other organizational situations.

- Manage to lead by discovering time. Have fewer meetings and focus those meetings on inquiry. A principal can develop school schedules that provide opportunities for groups of teachers to meet with and at times, to meet without the principal. Learn to depend upon e-mail and memos to limit the amount of time at faculty meetings or the number of faculty meetings dedicated to routine announcements. If you can say it in a memo—do so. Save valuable meeting time for inquiry.
- Consider the size and needs of different groups. A small school can engage all faculty members in one meeting. The author has facilitated successful sessions with as many as thirty teachers. However, larger faculties require different meeting strategies. Grade-level groups in elementary schools and departments in secondary schools provide smaller but natural groups. Also, there are times when it is important to put people in groups in which they do not normally communicate, such as groups of math,

science, English, foreign language, health, P.E., and other teachers. Such groupings tend to generate broader dialogue.
- Consider the comfort levels of participants. A beginning could be to meet with teachers in grade-level groups. As they become comfortable in sharing in this format, initiate meetings with the entire faculty. This is a long process. Focus on slowly drawing out teachers' opinions. Teacher comfort and voice are your guides. You will make many mistakes along the way, but persist. Acknowledge your mistakes; that acknowledgment frees other participants to risk change. Remember, influencing change, rather than controlling, is what leaders do.
- Begin your work by asking for participants' help. Explain your intent to begin an open inquiry process. Share your plan to reduce the number of meetings and the way you will do this. Use Isaacs's (1999a; 1999b) four practices or similar tools as the ground rules for the conversations. During the conversations, your job is to enforce the ground rules, but do so gently. For example, if someone continually interrupts others to speak, then you must manage the conversation by asking others to speak. At times you may need to approach an over-active participant after a conversation and ask him or her to help you encourage others to speak.
- Help participants understand that in the inquiry meetings the principal, or other formal leader, is not a decision-making agent, but a learner and facilitator for the learning of participants and herself or himself. Explain that you know that all participants have unique knowledge and wisdom to share, and hope that they will choose to do so. This role is powerful, but only works if participants truly trust that whatever views are expressed will be accepted with no retribution either in the meeting or later.
- Ask teachers to help you honor the rules and thank them when they do so. It requires courage to thank another person for correcting you for violating a rule. Your teaching in this situation is thanking another for helping you learn: an act of leadership.
- Ask participants to openly discuss their beliefs about teaching and learning. Ask them to critique programs and policies. This is slow and deliberate work. Carefully plan your participation so that it is safe for all participants to openly and honestly express themselves. The formal leader should not give voice to her or his ideas until it is clear that all participants feel safe when they speak.
- When you speak, focus upon how teachers' views are contributing to your learning. Remember, this is a democratic process—you want to learn from participants and for them to feel that it is safe to learn from each other and from you. Regardless of your own thoughts, listen for the truth in the speaker's words. It is the speaker's truth. Focus on understanding at a factual and emotional level.

- There are no sacred cows: for you or others. You will likely hear some things that make you uncomfortable. That is good. Acknowledge your discomfort, but don't defend.
- Facilitate so that all can listen and so that all can speak, but are not required to do so. Some individuals learn best by sharing, others by listening. Some individuals just need more time and others are simply shy about speaking out but reflect deeply on the conversation. Often, these deeply reflective individuals come up with the most significant ideas. Some teachers will sit quietly throughout a conversation and send you a note or an e-mail later on expressing their ideas, fears, and concerns.
- Take notes or ask someone to take notes at the meetings. Summarize the notes and send the summary to participants asking if the summary is accurate. Use feedback to adjust the summary. Add those late ideas sent to you after the meeting(s), but only after you have obtained permission from the sender to do so. Otherwise you are violating a trust.
- If you need to divide into groups for inquiry meetings, then send copies of all feedback to teachers of each group and send a summary of each meeting to all participants. This practice of transparency elevates the conversation in the meetings to a public level, enhancing individual responsibility and honoring the open spirit of inquiry. It is a way of telling participants that their words have value, including the opinions of those with whom you may disagree.
- Be willing to challenge policies and decisions made by a central authority when it is clear that such a policy or procedure is not in the interests of those the policy is intended to serve. This is a test of trustworthiness. Failure to honor this moral responsibility will always sabotage communication for the entire organization, including central authority.
- Understand that pursuing wisdom through open inquiry is an ongoing process. You will collectively make decisions that are long lasting and you will individually make better decisions based on the knowledge you gain from participants. Also, the learning that occurs as a result of successful inquiry processes over time reduces the necessity for formal leader decision making. Participants develop greater agency: their individual leadership capacity improves. They become more competent and responsible.
- Decisions developed through inquiry are not permanent. There is never room for "we have always done it this way." It is important to review prior decisions, current practice, and beliefs, including the mission/vision of the organization. This is *LTL* practice at the heart of the notion of a learning organization, and an ongoing action research process for continuous improvement.

Chapter 7
MAKING ACTION RESEARCH REAL

Rowden's four stages of strategic planning and how each subsequent stage involved greater numbers of an organization's participants were presented in chapter 5. Phase 1 was a purely traditional, positivist, top-down view. Leaders would analyze objective data, develop solutions, and apply these fixes to the organization. Phase 2 developed in response to the failure of the initial top-down initiatives. These positivist leaders were unable to bring about the changes they desired within their organizations because they were limited by their own knowledge and perceptions of reality.

In phase 2, realizing the need for broader leadership participation, middle managers were engaged in implementing solutions. In phase 3, top management focused on the need to "sell" their solutions to an even broader group of the organization's participants. In other words, each phase gave the appearance of more democratic engagement of a wider variety of participants, but only to problems defined or identified by centralized management.

In most schools and school systems, we are still very engaged with the application of phase 3 strategies. Teachers have some say about how they apply solutions to management-identified problems. But this management constructed, problem generating framework is too narrow. Phase 3 strategic planning when applied in schools universally identifies low test scores as "the" problem that must be addressed and engages teachers in investigating ways the scores can be improved. This is an attempt to engage school staffs in action research, and to some extent, this works.

Engaging teachers in action research projects that analyze tests results and apply those findings to instruction can help raise test scores. But this is a temporary trap, reflecting positivist *now* thinking. Low test scores are only symptoms of larger economic and social problems. Raising scores does not necessarily address those larger problems and can actually contribute to them. What typically happens is that the focus on testing leads to narrower instruction as more and more emphasis is placed on addressing the curriculum items that are tested.

Consequently, the test focus moves away from addressing the complex higher-order thinking and learning skills that students really need for success in their transition to higher levels in school. Paradoxically, engagement with higher-order thinking and learning activities will ultimately generate higher test scores. But much more importantly, a focus on higher-order thinking and learning assessment and teaching helps generate the complex skill development that students will need once they leave school and join the adult world.

The *narrow-now* solution focusing only on test scores reflects Peter Senge's (1990) "Laws of the Fifth Discipline" (p. 57). The first law was "Today's problems come from yesterday's solutions" (p. 57) and the third law was "Behavior grows better before it grows worse" (p. 60). A more realistic assessment would suggest that low test scores are not the problem but a symptom of a deeper problem: the need for students to develop a better understanding of and deeper meaning from the curriculum.

The flaw with phase 3 strategic planning is that, just as in phases 1 and 2, a centralized power source identifies the problem: test scores are not high enough. Consequently, teachers are held accountable for improving test scores. What happens? They play a game where they respond to mandates but are not committed to them. They comply, follow the rules, and deliver performance at the minimally acceptable rate. These teachers are received knowers unable to develop a moral and ethical responsibility that encourages them to stretch student learning beyond the acceptable test level. They are accountable but not responsible.

However, good teachers, and that is most teachers, attempt to maintain a sense of responsibility for students and covertly teach a curriculum they individually believe is more suited to the needs of their students. They continually struggle to balance organizational accountability demands with individual professional responsibility. Often, they must secretly sabotage policy to successfully achieve what they see as their moral and ethical obligations as professional teachers.

An example in chapter 5 recounted the author's recognition that it was morally appropriate for teachers to disobey his instruction to stop teaching phonics because the district had adopted a whole language school framework. Such sabotage is not only common among good teachers in schools, but an essential ingredient for the success of any school. System success depends upon teachers' responsibility much more than accountability. Indeed, there have been many instances where unions ask teachers to work to the specifications of district contracts and policies in lieu of more drastic actions. Teachers have usually won such contests.

However, individual teachers are limited in their ability to successfully demonstrate responsibility and improve student learning for two reasons. First, their knowledge is limited to their own classroom experiences, their own understanding of curriculum, and their own skills and attributes. Second, lone teachers have very limited voice. Teachers together have much greater ability to improve a school than do teachers working alone.

Together, they can be heard by one another and by their leader. Additionally, if the principal is doing a good job of representing the teachers with whom she or he works, teachers will be heard by central office as well. Teachers learn from and with one another, and their lessons have value for everyone. They become more focused on a shared goal and move toward the achievement of that goal together rather than working toward individual goals that are often in conflict with the goals of others.

Teachers in many schools have been able to successfully meet mandates and secretly maintain their professional independence. However, as testing requirements have become more intrusive, maintaining this balance is becoming more and more difficult. Policy makers and managers of accountability systems have become increasingly effective in inventing and identifying standardizing tactics that focus more and more on inspecting teacher work and increasingly requiring teachers to focus on narrowly tested curriculum elements.

This would be fine if the tested elements accurately represented the knowledge our students need, but this is a largely unsupported and unproven assumption. Policies that enhance accountability have been increasing for the past thirty years. These increasingly complicated accountability rules have the effect of focusing instruction on narrow and isolated bits of knowledge: the items that are tested. These policies have not substantially impacted the gaps between rich and poor, or reduced the number of children in poverty. These machine-age school improvement tactics increase the quantity of management but not the quality of teaching.

Unfortunately, as inspection increases, sharing decreases. For example, more and more districts and states, including the author's own state of Tennessee, are providing incentives for obtaining higher test scores and removing those teachers whose scores don't go up. A word, borrowed from marketing, has been used extensively to describe this effort. This word is *incentivize*. Positivist-thinking market oriented advocates believe that "incentivizing" teachers to improve test scores is the key to educational *reform*.

THE TENNESSEE MISTAKE

Tennessee's *First to the Top* (2010) grant includes a new teacher evaluation system. This new system provides a good example of the negative consequences of a successful positivist policy and our local version of incentivizing teachers. Thirty-five percent of the scoring of this new system depends on each teacher's student scores on the Tennessee Value Added Assessment System (*First to the Top*, 2010).

Theoretically, this system measures student learning growth from one year to the next. However, there will be at least two important negative outcomes if the system planners who created this complicated positivist solution have correctly calculated that they can get teachers to forgo the social norms and professional responsibility that have always guided them in exchange for market norms and financial incentives.

First, teachers will be focused primarily upon getting high test scores. Consequently, they will be less likely to share instructional strategies with other grade-level teachers. They will individually own and protect those successful strategies because they will be in competition with other teachers. Second, teachers will have little incentive to provide the support that might help a teacher in the previous grade because lower scores for incoming students mean better opportunities to raise scores in an individual teacher's class.

This competition is in direct contrast to the traditional interest in, but limited opportunity, that teachers have always had in supporting the teachers of their future students. Before value-added systems, teachers wanted students to come into their classrooms as well prepared as possible. For incentivized teachers, high-performing students become a liability because they are statistically not as likely to show as much improvement as underperforming students. Each teacher will be competing in a value-added test-invented market with other teachers in the school.

Such a system cannot lead to excellence. This seems similar to Wall Street's newest invention: market derivatives—a system devised to earn money for those who generate the derivatives that has little if any value for the people in the marketplace. For Tennessee's schools, everyone is caught in a vicious cycle of increasing dependence on carrots and sticks for a problem perceived and invented by those in positions of policy-making authority. The problem is that the policy maker's invented problem and market-based solution works against the interests of students, teachers, and communities— including the larger American community.

We have invented a system that makes a victim of everyone except the policy maker, who keeps reinventing the problem because it is good politics, and the test creator, who for substantial reward is continually incentivized to verify the policy. Quoting Senge (1990) once again, "The cure can be worse than the disease" creating an addictive solution that generates an "increased need for more and more of the solution" (p. 61).

The core problem is that level 3 strategic planning is missing an essential step: the one step that can move a school and school district into becoming a learning organization—an organization driven by the social norms of care and responsibility. It is missing a process of open inquiry that can contribute to the natural *LTL* characteristics of the school. Engaging teachers in phase 3 strategic planning problem solving is a form of limited inquiry, generally referred to today as action research.

Action research is an important and useful set of tools that become essential for focused inquiry when it arises as a product of open inquiry. But action research is a phase 3 strategic planning practice when it is applied as a tool for solving a problem identified by an organization's management, whether that management is in central office, the state house, or the nation's capital.

When applied in schools, phase 3 action research is a manipulation designed to obtain support for solutions to problems that teachers don't necessarily believe are real or solvable. The solutions developed in this manner tend to be superficial and teachers' commitment to implement them successfully is limited. Teachers become accountable but not necessarily responsible.

Problems identified through open inquiry are not just management concerns. Open inquiry moves an organization from level 3 strategic planning to level 4 because it moves the problem identification process from a central authority and gives it to the entire organization. There is a strong possibility that a problem so identified will be closer to reality than a management identified derivative. Consequently, problems identified through inquiry become challenges shared by all participants. Open inquiry changes an organization's participants from being accountable workers to becoming responsible agents. Participants are not *gaming*; they are living.

Teachers participating in an environment grounded in open inquiry become responsible for their work, for one another, and most importantly for their students. They move away from responding to carrot and stick motivation carried in from the norms of markets and begin responding to higher-order, social norm factors. They develop a culture of care, support, and learning.

Problems identified by a school's participants as a product of open inquiry can use action research strategies to develop solutions with greater possibilities for success. A problem identified through open inquiry becomes the natural spotlight for focused inquiry/action research. Working to develop solutions to such problems become responsibilities for the community. The whole organization becomes responsible for creating solutions and committed to making the solutions work, and they do so in collaboration rather than in competition.

In the responsible agency-honoring *LTL* environment, the transition from open inquiry to focused inquiry/action research occurs naturally as participants surface their individual voices and develop a collective voice; the real mission and vision of the school. They surface their individual voices and, through open inquiry, develop a collective voice so that they know who they are as a collaborative and as an organization.

Once a faculty collectively establishes who they are and what they believe, they are in a position to address successfully why test scores might be low. They might discover that flaws in their teaching are preventing students from learning what they need to know. Actually, in true effective *LTL* environments, teachers know well before standardized tests are taken what gaps exist in student learning and will have begun working to address them.

Additionally, they may discover that the tests don't examine what students need to know. If they make this discovery, then the school principal has a responsibility to collaborate with other school principals and address this issue with central office, and the school superintendent has a responsibility to collaborate with other superintendents and address this issue with the state department of education. To do less would likely meet accountability mandates but certainly would not meet the moral and ethical responsibilities of professionals. The *LTL* environment generates a culture of discovery. Teachers may discover that their emphasis on improving test results is interfering with their instruction of the higher-order thinking and learning skills in which students need to engage so that they may be successful at subsequent grades. The teachers might discover that issues outside of school are interfering. They might discover that there are actions they and/or their principals can take to engage the community and address some of those factors.

It is likely that teachers will discover a combination of issues and factors that interfere with student learning. In other words, they will examine and develop understandings of the complex issues they experience daily and be better able to address those issues. They will believe in their abilities and actually be empowered to address these issues. Engaging as responsible agents, they will collectively become a learning organization. Indeed, the nation of Finland has built its successful educational program by emphasizing teacher responsibility and professionalism.

AUTHENTIC ACTION RESEARCH

Action research strategies have many advocates, such as Sagor (2000) and McNiff and Whitehead (2006). Although different practitioners have additional steps, at its core, action research has four basic steps. It begins with identifying and studying a problem, then taking some action to address the problem, evaluating the outcome, and reflecting on what has been learned in the process. Then, as it is a continuous process, the cycle begins again. It can be practiced by an individual teacher, a single school, or an entire district. However, action research becomes focused inquiry when the identification of a problem comes about as a product of open inquiry.

In phase 3 strategic planning, step 1, the identification and study phase, is completed by someone in a position of authority. In focused inquiry, the participants of the organization have completed that step and it has come from their open inquiry processes. Consequently, the participants feel responsible for the problem, responsible for finding a solution, responsible for making the solution work, and able to learn from the process.

Open inquiry provides opportunities for schools to operate as true learning organizations and "learn" their purposes for themselves. Having learned this, they can focus inquiry upon discovering the specific obstacles that interfere with achieving their purposes and develop responsible practices for overcoming those obstacles. Such schools contribute to better futures for the communities they serve.

This is infinitely more powerful than participant accountability. Participants in such a learning organization find the process itself rewarding, motivating, and renewing. Please notice, no coins are used in this work. It is not market driven: it is social responsibility grounded in an ethic of care. Also note that this is not saying teacher pay is not important. It is for two reasons. A higher salary is an indicator of how well a society values teachers' work. People who believe their work is valued are better performers. Second, well-paid teachers are better able to focus on the needs of students. After all, the nations that highly value teachers have the best schools.

SEEKING WISDOM AS COMMUNITY

This chapter has been about challenging modern positivist thinking and seeking wisdom by developing *LTL* attributes through *open inquiry* grounded in open dialogue and productive discussion. The primary purpose was to present a way to address and overcome the inertia of the limitations of the thinking left over from the age of industrialization. The *LTL* framework suggests a new placement of schools in our social structure, and a revaluing of education and educators.

Wisdom-seeking school leaders will continue to make decisions and give direction, which are required management functions. However, within the wisdom-seeking, *LTL* framework, the principal and other school leaders will also develop roles as facilitators of inquiry. These individuals manage to lead. They become initiators of and models for streams of adaptation, change, and organizational evolution. They can accomplish much more than mere managers of a stagnant status quo.

The power of these roles lies in the possibility of creating deep understandings of the shared responsibilities every school participant has for the learning of each student and for enabling that student to become a capable and successful participant in the community. This is citizenship responsibility at the core of teacher professionalism—behaviors that educators can and should model for society. This leadership can serve as the model that can guide our divided society toward the respectful unity needed to make the changes the future will demand. But constructing a wisdom-seeking *LTL* organization requires leaders who first develop themselves.

Chapter Eight

Constructing Self, Constructing Organization

A focus of chapter 3 was on how we humans construct individual views of the world. This was explained in terms of a metaphorical cabin that contains our thinking. We share our thinking and influence one another through the doors and windows of the cabin and use a mirror to examine our own thinking. The metaphorical cabin containing our constructed vision of reality is also a good way to think about how we create functional organized systems. All human organizations are socially constructed, complex systems.

Our abilities to share our complex thinking with others are interactions that make us unique among living things. We humans have been visiting one another's thought cabins for thousands of years and consequently have developed very similar cabins. These shared beliefs are contained in the cabin of thought that each of us builds and, hopefully, remodels when we realize that our experiences and shared perceptions are proving our assumptions untrue. In other words, we are not limited to what we think. We can change and must do so in order to survive. These thinking changes are the product of *LTL*.

Actually, thought caves or thought castles might have been good metaphors because both structures likely predate log cabins. Terms such as grass hut, mud hut, or yurt could have been used. However, log cabins seem appropriate for Americans: just the perfect pragmatic and constructivist icon bringing to mind Henry David Thoreau, David Crockett, and Abraham Lincoln. It also brings to mind the challenge of *Uncle Tom's Cabin*. Isn't it amazing that you are reading these words, understanding them, and able to compare their meaning to the content of your thinking cabin, hut, or yurt? Are we not an interesting species?

Chapter 8
PLAYING AND KNOWING RESPONSIBILITY

Constructivism has become both a philosophy of education and a science within education. Every individual comes to know reality by constructing or creating a unique framework of understanding. Our shared understanding of this thinking framework came about through many years of work by a wide variety of thinkers, scientists, and teachers. Perhaps the most important was the work of philosopher and educator John Dewey, one of the pioneers of progressivism. His work extended from early in the twentieth century into the 1940s.

Other important figures include Lev Vygotsky and Jean Piaget. Vygotsky, a Russian psychologist, worked in the 1920s and 1930s. He developed important theories including the zone of proximal development, which identifies the range of learning available to a learner. Jean Piaget, a Swiss biologist, is generally considered the direct father of constructivist science. He developed the theory of cognitive development that has been the basis of our understanding of the stages of knowledge that develop in each individual.

One of the interesting and significant perspectives shared by these pioneering scientists and thinkers is one that we seem to have recently forgotten in our discussion of schooling. It has to do with the importance of play. These theorists and researchers all viewed play as a central feature in the development of a child's cognition. They understood that play is the process through which humans and higher-order animals develop cognition or knowledge and understanding.

Through play we humans develop an abstract understanding of the world. The most rewarding part of the author's childhood occurred in the mountains and deserts of northwestern New Mexico. His friends were Jicarilla Apaches and children whose ancestors had been Spanish settlers from the sixteenth and seventeenth centuries. Play centered on fishing, camping, building rafts to float down the river, and exploring mountain plateaus and glorious sandstone formations. The author and his playmates spent a good deal of playtime pretending to be cowboys, vaqueros, or native warriors. These experiences generated a deep love of wild places and a valuing of human difference.

Play was central to the author's development as an individual. It invented the individual as he was inventing it. What about you? What did you play growing up? What did you imagine? How did your play shape you? This is where the notion of the term "constructivist" comes in. We humans develop or construct an abstract representation of the elements of the world in our minds. In essence, we each internally develop a play or imaginary world: the thought cabins described earlier.

There seem to be two elements related to play that make it so essential. One of the things that make us humans different from other living creatures is our ability to communicate abstract notions and thereby co-construct worldly representations. That is, we make individual constructions that are quite similar to the constructions of others. We play together. We invent as we are being invented. These dynamic and continuously changing events have enabled our social evolution.

Another aspect of play is developing possibilities: the prerequisite for the requisite variety that enables us to adapt to changing environments. It is the process of creation, of becoming unique individuals. This quality of play contains our ability to learn: a characteristic of nature that we humans latched onto that has been responsible for our ascendency as a species and for the ascendency of the American nation. It is also the feature that modern, positivist, *now and narrow thinking* denies.

Those who make and regulate school policy don't seem to understand that knowledge must be constructed. Our standardized testing and teaching practices rest upon a false foundation: a hidden assumption that denies the basic human connection between play and learning. The untrue assumption is that we can just tell people something and they will know it. We can build on our knowledge by receiving information but only to the extent that we have the experiential background to have constructed a frame upon which we can attach the new information. In other words, learning occurs best during play.

Here is one example. The author had an ablation procedure to correct a rapid and irregular heartbeat at the Cleveland clinic. The electrophysiologist provided a report for the author's hometown physician. Although recognizing every word, the author was unable to comprehend the meaning assigned to the words as they were organized in the report. This document was clearly, as Vygotsky would have said, not within the author's zone of proximal development. The doctor who had written the report and the doctor for whom it was intended had through many years constructed a shared world that the author did not understand.

These doctors had spent a great deal of time at play. But wait, are you thinking of this as the work of these doctors? Was it? You have likely heard that "a child's work is play." Perhaps adults are not different. When does play become work? When should play become work? A house cleaner was preparing to clean the hotel room as the author and his wife were leaving for the hospital. She appeared to be hot, tired, and basically miserable as she finished the room next door. She was clearly working, but her work did not appear to be at all similar to the work of the surgical team encountered later that day at the clinic.

The author was awake throughout the ablation operation. Tiny wires were inserted from the patient's groin into his heart. Looking at a giant television screen, the electrophysiologist moved the wires to different sections of the atrial chambers and triggered irregular heartbeats. He would then zap those few cells electrically and return the author's heart rate to normal sinus rhythm. Sorry, this is likely more than you want to know about this procedure, but this helps illustrate the point about work and play.

Yes, this highly skilled surgeon was working, as were the five other expert individuals in attendance. But they were also playing. They seemed thoroughly engaged and even entertained by the activity. Watching their work, the author visualized Captain Kirk and his team of officers aboard the Starship Enterprise exploring new parts of the universe. This surgical team may have been at work, but they were also at play.

The essential difference between the surgical team's work and a group of kids imagining themselves on a starship, performing on a stage, participating in an imaginary tea party, engaged in a video game, or playing vaqueros and native warriors is *responsibility*. The surgical team members were individually and collectively responsible for a life. Indeed, the life at stake was from at least one perspective very important.

Yes, the surgical team was accountable for their performance, as was the hotel housekeeper. But there is an important difference between the housekeeper and the surgical team members. The housekeeper's supervisor was inspecting the room next door and finding fault with the housekeeper's performance as the author left the hotel. The surgical team that was responsible for a life had no such inspector. They needed no such inspector. They were motivated by the challenging nature of the task itself and the responsibility they felt for a life. Consequently, they were engaged like actors on a stage, but their performances were very real.

It is difficult to imagine that some system that merely held these doctors and nurses accountable for their work could possibly inspire them to seek such high levels of responsibility. Certainly, these individuals got to participate on this elite team through a great deal of hard work. But this work included a good deal of mind play. Each individual on this team of specialists must have performed parts of this operation many times, taking an imaginary story and making it a real event. Isn't this what we call play? Don't successful athletes imagine themselves performing as a normal part of their training? What about stage performers?

Additionally, the mind play displayed by the members of this surgical team had strong connections to each individual member's sense of right and wrong. Whenever humans imagine themselves in situations they are typically heroes. Of course, the hero always chooses the right ethical and moral path. These medical specialists were engaged with one another in creating and living a hero's journey. They were choosing responsibility.

So, let's add one more important aspect of play. We act out heroic characters as an important part of our development. We spend an enormous amount of time in imaginary, creative play and daydream that we are heroes of the stories we create. Think about your childhood. Surely you played imaginary characters and it is likely that most of your characters were heroic: maybe

Superman, Robin Hood, Annie Oakley, a teacher in a garage set up as a classroom, or Mommy and Daddy in a room with dolls. The argument here is that imaginary play is the basis for the enhancement of creativity and heroic play for the development of responsibility.

What about you? What part of your work is play? What do you do that is a product of what you have first imagined? Do you turn elements of your work into play? Are you the hero of your stories? The desire to be the heroes of our stories, that is, the acceptance of moral and ethical responsibility, is a much more powerful control over individual and collective behavior than any externally managed modern accountability mechanism could possibly deliver.

Moral and ethical responsibility is developed through our play and imagination. We develop responsibility because we need to be heroes. The author's experiences as a principal have led to understanding that at least one reason people choose to become teachers is the human desire to be heroes. The desire to be the heroes of our stories is the backdrop for successful human connection. We practice responsibility through play, have lived it as parents for thousands and perhaps millions of years, and have extended this ministerial practice beyond the family to professional service.

One more story piece from this hospital adventure. The day following surgery, the author was officially released from care, but unable to leave the hospital. It seemed his clothing had been misplaced. He was not particularly happy about the idea of getting into a cab in an open-backed hospital gown. Please accept his apology for enabling you to imagine this rather unpleasant thought. After several anxious minutes of waiting, the head nurse from the surgical team flew into the room with a plastic bag containing the clothes.

During the surgery, this nurse had engaged the author in conversation to keep him calm but awake, both essential for the success of the surgery and clearly an important part of her performance. Breathing heavily, she entered his room with the missing bag of clothing. Needing to get back to the operating theater quickly, she had run several flights of stairs and numerous corridors from the electrophysiology lab to the recovery wing. She was not accountable for this clothing or for getting the articles to their owner, but took on this task because she was a responsible agent. The author thanked her and said she was his hero and an excellent teacher.

Most educators have until recently believed that the transition from work to play is a gradual one that occurs at some point in the transition from childhood to adulthood. You have likely heard the old adage that "All work and no play makes Jack a dull boy." In the machine age we traded away the ideas of play, learning, and pursuing knowledge for a more secure economic well-being. And it worked. But the parameters of modernity focused on *now* and *narrow* thinking are limiting our future—including our economic future.

We are reaching the limits of the usefulness of the machine age; those limits are making us dull of both heart and mind.

If necessity is the mother of invention, then play must be the father. America was built on play. We have continually engaged in imaginary events that we have brought into the real world. Our inventions were first created in a state of play, including the foundation of the nation itself. It was imagined before it was real. It came about because the inventors tried something new, and took some risk. *Now* and *narrow*, the entities of the Neverland created in modernity, allow none of that.

Neverland thinking insists that we engage only that which is perceived as tried and true and not something new. *Now* and *narrow* are monsters we have constructed that thrive on fear: fear that thrives on accountability systems, but abhors responsible agents. Fear that prevents us from exploring, discovering, inventing, and creating. This fear encroaches on the natural tendency of all humans, but especially our young, to play, to learn, and to become responsible. We are setting about making all children dull of heart and mind.

SCHOOLS ARE COMPLEX SYSTEMS

All systems are combinations of individual parts that have become organized to achieve some purpose. Right now, the author is sitting on a simple single-purpose system, organized by someone in a carpentry workshop. It is nearly identical to five additional structures that look attractive and welcoming around the dining room table. This system is essentially a group of sticks extending above and below a flat piece of wood indented to fit rather nicely around a derriere. It is easily recognizable to most humans as a chair.

The title *chair* was assigned to this system by a much more complex system, evolved by humans long ago: the English language. Of course, the system we call the English language is not static. It continues to change. Apparently, so does the system we call *chair*. The salesman who sold the author and his wife the dining room chairs tried to sell a soft recliner that would provide a massage. However, that complicated chair system was more evolved and expensive than the author's wife would allow. She would not accept the rationale that the recliner was appropriate for the author's evolving body.

The primary subject of this text is a system that is much more complex and abstract than a chair. This system is perhaps as complex as the English language. It is the school: a primary organizing system that has evolved to enable the rich and sophisticated development of human society. This system is of fairly recent human construction and represents the pinnacle of human organizational achievement.

This system can be a specific school as in the statement, "My grandson is a second grader in school." It can refer to schools generally, as in, "Our school system needs money." Or it can refer to schools more globally as in "Our schools are failing." Of these three statements, the first is true. Well, it was true when it was written, but by the time you read it, the author's grandson may be in third or even fourth grade. The second statement is also true, and the third represents the misperception that inspired this book.

So, just what are schools as "systems?" What ends do they serve? Let's see if we can answer these questions. A system is an organization of parts. It is organized because the parts are related. If each part of the system has few parts, it is a simple system. If it has many parts, it may be described as complicated. Regardless of the number of pieces making up the system, if each is related to one or more other parts in only one way, then the system is complicated.

If the parts are related to other parts in more than one way, then the system is complex. Complexity is a central element in understanding all human organization. What are the parts of an organization we call school? Obviously, schools have nonliving, simple, and complicated elements like books, desks, buildings, playground equipment, and hopefully, a sufficient supply of soap and paper goods in the washroom.

Traditionally, the job of running the school, that is, keeping the organization functioning, had to do with managing these elements. A principal with whom the author worked several years ago described his job as handling the three B's: books, budgets, and balls. But these are the physical elements that go with schools. They tend to be complicated and require managing. After all, it is essential to have the necessary books and balls, and it is very important to have a budget that provides for these items. These days, we also need to add computers, software, and technology training to that list. Of course, books may soon become passé.

However, what truly makes a school are people: students, parents, teachers, a principal or principals, custodians, community members, and the neighbors across the street who are hopefully not very concerned when a grandson and his friends walk through their flower beds. It is people who started the school to serve the needs of the children who arrive at the school each day, so that when the students leave a few years later, they will help the people who started the school, and eventually help re-create that school or other schools, and so on.

Theoretically, a school is a self-sustaining, self-renewing, organized, complex system, purposed to support the larger organization that sponsors it: the community. The system's parts or members are students, teachers, principals, and others. These parts are helped and encouraged to acquire greater skills and knowledge. Hopefully, the skills and knowledge acquired from schooling enables them to seek wisdom as well.

What makes the school self-sustaining and self-renewing is the ability of the complex members of the system to adapt and change. As these members adapt and change individually, they are also evolving the system. Please note that adaptation, change, and evolution are presented as synonymous terms in this text. So, we need to have a framework to understand what human organizational evolution looks like.

How do the individuals in an organization evolve so that they are able to make adaptations to meet the needs of the organization and the people it serves in a continually changing environment? We could just as easily say: How do the individuals in an organization adapt so that they are able to make changes to meet the needs of the organization and the people it serves in a continuously evolving environment?

WHY DEVELOP EMPOWERMENT?

The author's discovery and application of the work of Mary Belenky et al. (1997) was introduced in chapter 1. Belenky and her colleagues analyzed the self-perception of economically poor and disempowered mothers, as they participated in dialogue groups. They traced the women's growth as they moved from being totally dependent upon others as sources of knowledge to recognizing their individual agency in the construction of self-understanding. Over time, these women developed a sense of themselves and their ability to learn. That is, they became more empowered.

The Belenky framework contains five classifications representing a continuum of increasing self-knowledge. At the lowest level are silenced individuals who do not understand that they can have knowledge, ideas, or opinions. They believe all knowledge comes from others. A more highly developed level of self-knowledge is received knowing. Such individuals realize that they can understand the knowledge that they have received from others. Such individuals can only receive knowledge and be held accountable to others. They do not construct or create knowledge and do not understand that responsibility is a personal attribute.

Three levels represent increasing levels of responsibility. The subjective knower recognizes self-ability to question and evaluate knowledge presented by others, and the procedural knower recognizes her individual agency in adapting procedures developed by others to meet the needs of self and of others. The highest level of self-perception in the Belenky framework is constructed knowing: Such individuals recognize that their ability to construct knowledge for themselves is the same process that others use for generating knowledge, and they clearly recognize their moral and ethical responsibility for the actions they take.

The work of Belenky et al. is intriguing because of the strong parallels between their framework representing disempowered, impoverished mothers and the relationship that teachers have with the schools and communities in which they work. Teachers are disempowered members in a predominantly female profession, where decision making has traditionally been the purview of males. Analyzing the transcripts of the dialogue sessions the author sponsored for the teachers at Aspen Elementary School in reference to the Belenky et al. framework (Glover, 2003) confirmed and expanded his thinking.

The Belenky framework provided a useful tool for helping understand the teachers' perceptions of themselves, the school, and the school system. Consequently, the Belenky labels were adopted to develop a conceptual framework for how teachers view their relationships with the school and the larger society they serve. It is labeled *Developmental Empowerment (DE)*. Please see figure 8.1.

The *DE* analysis at Aspen clearly demonstrated that the relationships between the teachers and the elements of the school, school system, and the community were complex. When elements of discussion were about teachers' classrooms and their students, the teachers expressed opinions and views that revealed their perceptions of themselves as procedural knowers and constructed knowers. However, as the conversation moved away from items closely related to classroom work, the teachers' self-views were more representative of the subjective and received knower categories.

In other words, the teachers had sophisticated constructions of themselves and their roles in classrooms. They recognized their ability to influence what happened for and with the children they served. But as discussion moved beyond the classroom, the teachers' self-perceptions became less constructed. They tended to see themselves, their students, and their classrooms more as objects of the will and power of others. They saw themselves as disempowered objects who were held accountable for their students' performance, but felt responsible for their learning.

Below are some examples taken from teacher statements made in the dialogue sessions at Aspen School that illustrate the teachers' perceptions of their levels of empowerment. These statements represent the received knower (RK), subjective knower (SK), procedural knower (PK), and constructed knower (CK).

> Statement #1: My role is to teach children how to learn, not just specifics, but how to find and use knowledge and how to be part of a productive society (PK). We also teach part of the parents' job: manners, sex education, drug education, and more. We have to do this because I'm scared of what might happen if we don't (CK).
> Statement #2: To help children become well rounded citizens, we get flak for taking on more and more. Kids need to read, to understand, to communicate orally and in writing, work with others, and work a computer (PK). We keep

Teachers' Views of Self in Constructing the Teaching Profession:

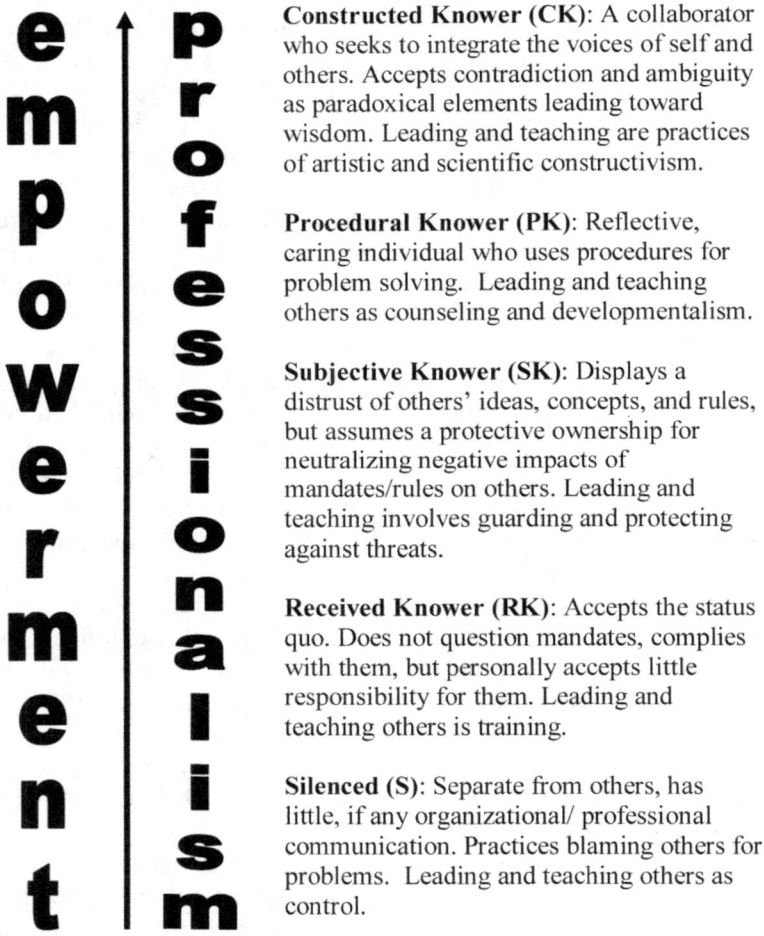

Constructed Knower (CK): A collaborator who seeks to integrate the voices of self and others. Accepts contradiction and ambiguity as paradoxical elements leading toward wisdom. Leading and teaching are practices of artistic and scientific constructivism.

Procedural Knower (PK): Reflective, caring individual who uses procedures for problem solving. Leading and teaching others as counseling and developmentalism.

Subjective Knower (SK): Displays a distrust of others' ideas, concepts, and rules, but assumes a protective ownership for neutralizing negative impacts of mandates/rules on others. Leading and teaching involves guarding and protecting against threats.

Received Knower (RK): Accepts the status quo. Does not question mandates, complies with them, but personally accepts little responsibility for them. Leading and teaching others is training.

Silenced (S): Separate from others, has little, if any organizational/ professional communication. Practices blaming others for problems. Leading and teaching others as control.

Figure 8.1. **Developmental Empowerment, a Theoretical Tool for Analyzing Teacher Growth.** *Source:* **Modified from Belenky et al. (1986, pp. 76–77).**

adding on more and more, and the joy is kind of drifting away because I can't do the special things I once did in my classroom. The kids miss out (RK). Statement #3: [We need to] give kids the skills to discover who they are (CK). We are successful with some and not with others (RK). But, I am here to teach children and not just [teach] subject matter. Everyone has a right to learn and they can do that in my classroom. We are giving them opportunities to be successful (SK).

Statement #4: [Our job is] to give each child a chance to be anything she or he wants to be (CK).
Statement #5: Its more than just basic skills, kids need to learn to be thinkers, to find and use knowledge (PK).
Statement #6: Public education takes pressure off families and puts it on society (RK).
Statement #7: To educate the population for our well-being (RK). But this isn't just about jobs. It is also about social needs. Our schools are not meeting the needs of children or matching them to jobs (SK).
Statement #8: We need to teach children to think, but we are moving away from that and worrying about testing (RK). (Glover, 2003, pp. 227–28)

No statements from the transcripts of the dialogue sessions were classified as representing characteristics of a silenced individual. But there were some teachers in the school where the author had previously served as principal who would be classified as silenced. Additionally, while serving as a consultant in other schools, the author has encountered silenced teachers. Unfortunately, many people he has encountered both in and out of schools could be classified as silenced. Sadly, these people have often been children.

For several years, the author simply accepted that teachers display greater agency, responsibility, and empowerment at the classroom level and less as conversation moves beyond the classroom, to the school and the community. It is certainly logical that we humans feel greater control over that which is close at hand. However, an important question surfaced over time. Should teachers have greater influence over the nature of their work?

Modern positivist organizations limit the empowerment that participants exhibit, because they are systems designed to be managed. One important function of positivistic thinking is to generate participant dependency upon those with power and authority for the knowledge required for decision making. Modern organizations are designed to be mechanistic, one-way, direction-giving systems that limit change possibilities to the values of superordinates: those who manage the organization.

Organizational purpose in the positivist design can only be top down. It comes from the managers who claim knowledge and have power in the organization rather than from the organization itself. As a devoted mover-shaker modern positivist principal, the author's assumption was that his direction was required for school improvement. The principal was the central cog in the machine and the sole initiator of the movement of the machine.

But the faculty at Aspen School challenged these assumptions. The author discovered that teachers felt voiceless in terms of the larger organization. He also discovered that the teachers had valuable knowledge that could and should be applied toward improving the school and the school district. They saw their students as subjects with individual needs and wants. The organization and its positivist leaders, including the author, could only see students and teachers as objects to be manipulated and not as self-energizing elements. Yes, the author discovered that he was the broken link. He was the problem: a modern positivistic manager.

Stated in systems science terms, modern schools have very poor feedback loops: an element essential for system adaptability. The feedback cycle seems most broken at the principal position level. It is wrong to assume that those who have achieved higher position levels within the organization have superior knowledge or better access to it. It is wrong to assume that central office knows more than teachers.

The school's management was the product of the principal's assumption of superior knowledge. The author unknowingly depended upon limiting teacher knowledge to the lower levels of the *Developmental Empowerment* knowledge hierarchy. As a modern positivist manager, he did not want teachers who were silenced and accepted little accountability for their students' learning. But in failing to recognize the limitations of his own knowing, he also did not want teachers who would question, challenge, or misapply the assumed superior knowledge of centralized authority. Such questioning, challenge, and adaptations are characteristics of responsible agents.

This explains why school reforms have continuously failed to deliver the improvements for which they were designed. Most teachers have an ethical moral framework that guides their practice. They exhibit more than mere accountability for student performance. They accept a broad responsibility for their students that is generally not recognized or attended to by reform agendas. Teachers often reject reforms for moral and ethical reasons that the assumption-blind modern system doesn't see or understand. Teachers must sabotage policy for the benefits of their students.

However, teachers are also isolated to the individual practices of their own teaching (Tye, 2000). They generally have very limited opportunities to witness the teaching practices of others, so teacher knowledge is limited to their individual experiences. Almost every teacher has experienced successions of magic bullet reforms designed as blanket fixes applied to entire schools and districts. But these reforms generally are poor fits for individual teachers, classrooms, and students.

After a few years of bullet reform experiences, most teachers become quite suspect of every new reform that comes along. Consequently, programs that could actually have some value are discounted upon arrival. Teachers have responded to increasing reform efforts with decreasing interest. The paradox here is that teachers' moral and ethical responsibilities interfere with positivist efforts to improve schools.

Unfortunately, the author's mistaken beliefs about the viability of positivist leadership are not unusual. Most principals, district administrators, superintendents, state department of education personnel, politicians, and business leaders have similar wrong beliefs. Many school administrators still believe that they or their superordinates have the knowledge needed to change their schools.

These well-meaning but mistaken individuals also believe in the great national assumption that our schools are failing. This assumption was challenged in chapters 4 and 6. Those individuals with power and authority have simply assigned this label to schools. Consequently brave individuals who have warned about standardizing curriculums, instruction, and assessment, and basing pay on external motivation schemes, are simply not heard. People like Thomas Armstrong, Gerald Bracey, Paul Houston, Alfie Kohn, Susan Ohanian, Diane Ravitch, Yong Zhao, and many others get marginalized in the education policy discussion.

Coming to understand that the *DE* framework applied to the author and other principals exposed the trap posed by modernity. Modern, positive, objective thinking hides our individual and collective potential. Organizational management schemes limit participant creativity. In effect, the author was a received knower principal, blinded by a perception that those organizational ranks above him represented superior knowledge.

The author's effort to serve as a mover-shaker principal who pushed and managed toward identified solutions did not work. The more closely teachers were managed and pushed, the less capable they would become as teachers, thereby limiting their students' learning. Pushing either increases dependence on management or generates a push-back resistance; both responses limit teachers' ability to lead, teach, and learn in their own classrooms. A perfectly managed modern school, which is the apparent goal of contemporary policies, is a school of sameness, disengagement, and discontent. It is a place of work with no play.

WISE LEADERS SABOTAGE SELECTIVELY

But what would happen if the author stopped managing and encouraged everyone to try anything and everything? What would happen if everyone was just "doin' their own thing?" What if a principal encouraged everyone to experiment in any way they wished, as much and as often as they wanted? Of course the result would be chaos. Indeed, in many ways, modern positivism has been a response to the chaos and confusion of previous times.

Modernity has represented a giant step forward. It has generated a highly efficient set of very productive systems. These systems include clocks, standardized parts, navigation and communication equipment, assembly lines, corporations, and organized systems of government that include representative democracy and bureaucracy: the complicated structures that support so much of our lives.

However, these modern standardized systems are designed like machines and depend upon some degree of automaticity. They do not change directions well. Today, our greatest threat to progress may be that modern organizational management systems are reaching or have reached their maximum level of usefulness. Our schools provide the ideal example. Sadly, those individuals who regulate and operate such systems are becoming more effective in managing schooling and limiting the requisite variety our children need for their future.

So, as principal of Aspen, the author tried to find a new path for understanding his relationship with and responsibility for the school. Could a principal serve as a manager creating a level of stability, routine, and comfort, and simultaneously generate a process for challenging stability, routine, and comfort? Could a principal safely sabotage the system so that the system can change, adapt, evolve, and hopefully improve?

Engaging teachers in inquiry is an avenue for bringing individual thinking and voice together so that participants discover mutual interests and identify shared goals. It provides a way to generate a local wisdom spoken with power and commitment. Inquiry provided a democratic way to bring a focus to the work of the school. Inquiry was a way to seek and develop the wisdom of the group that empowered participants to set and accomplish goals, to challenge ill-suited and even wrongheaded mandates, and to challenge one another to be better teachers in the school. Inquiry is an avenue for developing responsible agency.

The principal's role is to support the honest and authentic discovery of school purpose at the local level and to serve that purpose. The principal can provide the feedback loop that seems to be consistently missing from the modern positivist school organization. She can be the conduit for enabling teachers to collectively formulate their needs and beliefs into coherent messages and present those messages to central office. He can also interpret and explain the intent behind central office mandates. She can work in the school, work with other schools through relationships with principals and administrators, and reach out to work in the community.

The principal's role is to work toward developing a common organization vision shared by not only the teachers in the school, but by central office and the broader community. Within the accepted professional standards for educational leaders lies the justification for this work. The Interstate School Leaders License Consortium Standards provide the national framework for developing and evaluating school principals. The sixth and final standard is that "An education leader promotes the success of every student by understanding, responding to, and influencing the political, social, economic, legal, and cultural context" (Interstate School Leaders License Consortium Standards, 2008).

The principal's role is to serve as a teacher in and for the organization. Her or his value for the organization is the ability to provide the feedback link missing from the system. This is the essential missing element from the positivist framework. If a principal seeks wisdom, practices the *lead, teach, learn triad*, and truly honors the standards that guide the profession, then she or he must provide the feedback missing from the hierarchy of modernity that is essential for organizational change and success. The principal's role is to question and challenge the automaticity of modern schooling.

Could inquiry provide an organizational process that bridges the growing abyss between the rational and the spiritual, the external and the internal, the objective and the subjective that President Havel identified in his speech at Constitution Hall, quoted at the beginning of this text? Might this be the work that's needed to build the bridge that closes the gap between chaos and control?

Could democratic conversation deliver the variety necessary for generating future options and a way to select wisely from those options? Could this be the element that Havel suggested was being painfully born? Could an understanding and practice of a systemic feedback loop be the concept that would arise from the rubble? Can learning to value the thinking and beliefs of others allow a process for overcoming the separateness of modernity?

Chapter Nine

Choosing to Learn

This text presents a framework for rethinking the nature of leadership in schools and other organizations. It questions the assumptions we make about how we understand reality, who we are as participants in organizations, and the self-imposed limits we have acquired during the modern period. Modern thinking has allowed the construction of organizational structures to become entities that are superior to human beings. Consequently, we have made ourselves accountable to the needs of organizations rather than responsible for one another.

Modern self-imposed thinking limits are becoming increasingly dangerous for the future of our nation, our world, and our children. This final chapter addresses the nature of complex reality one more time. Although the *LTL* triad practices of leading, teaching, and learning are always difficult, they have provided the roadway for human social evolution and will continue to offer the best avenue toward a successful future.

These ideas about responsibility, motivation, the limits of knowledge, and seeking wisdom suggest a path for continuing to develop human success beyond the bonds and boundaries of modernity. The purpose is to challenge the limits of modern positive thinking and resurface the ancient process that has been responsible for successful human evolution: our natural urges to question and experiment. We can choose a learning path: to understand that what we know is always less than what we might know.

The evolutionary character of human progress paired with where we currently are on this continuous change path is an idea that requires additional discussion. Learning is becoming the primary feature of human organization. Consequently, our potential lies in our ability to challenge our knowing. As knowledge continues to evolve, challenges to knowing will become a more dominant feature of human relationships and greater necessity for organizational success.

However, knowing is a feature of power and it resists challenge. Inquiry is a natural challenge to power that has the capacity to enlist power sources themselves in making that challenge. The ability to enlist the power source depends upon the moral and ethical responsible agency of the inquirer and the power source. Learning is the outcome when this process is successful. That role is to challenge knowing and consequently, to challenge power. Teachers have always generated learning best with questions. The postmodern age provides an opportunity to enhance the role of the teacher as inquiry practitioner and learning organization leader.

SIMPLE EXQUISITE COMPLEXITY

Some lessons are very difficult to learn. One such lesson surfaced in a workshop designed to facilitate the development of a non-graded report card during the author's first principalship. A teacher with a rather narrow view of student motivation said, "You can't convince me that a child will do their [class] work if there is no grade for it." Remember, this was the school where the author played the role of a modern, instrumental, mover-shaker principal. In a knowing response to this question, the principal used every possible argument to prove that she was wrong. But she was right. Her mind was an impenetrable brick wall. She would not change her view.

Unfortunately, this discussion took up much of a busy in-service day, with a highly paid trainer standing around waiting. At first, the other teachers became irritated with this teacher. Then they became bored, and eventually, irritated with the author for arguing with her. What could have been a successful learning event for the faculty turned into a gripe session. This was not a fine leadership moment. It represented a difficult lesson to learn—so difficult that the author has continued to relearn this lesson for more than fifteen years. The lesson is that power fails at change: You simply cannot force another's change of mind.

Dan Ariely (2009) is correct: we are "predictably irrational." The author's grandfather would have added that "you can bring a horse to water but you can't make it drink." The same is true for people and ideas. Once you or just about anyone else has made up her or his mind about an issue, there is nothing another person can do to change that individual's thinking. The very best logical arguments will not prevail. So, whether you are a principal, teacher, parent, superintendent, general, corporate executive, or just about anyone else, anywhere, at any time, what can you do? You actually have, at most, four decision options.

First, if you are in a position of authority, you can force compliance. A manager has power to control the actions of others. A principal can force compliance with demands. But this would not change the complier's thinking. Instead, she or he will experience resentment for the leader and the organization. Of course, this limits the individual's successful functioning within the organization. In fact, forcing compliance likely causes a desire to want to sabotage a change agenda.

Actions of a participant in an organization can be managed, at least the ones a superordinate knows about. But no one can manage a participant's thinking. She or he is independent. So mandating action may be effective in the short run, such as a crisis or whenever an immediate action is required. But long-term dependence on mandates interferes with the participant support that organizations need for long-term growth and improvement. Mandates limit individual and organizational learning.

A second option is to just give up and say "have it your way." The author thinks of this as the Burger King option, but others call this laissez-faire management. Unfortunately, this is a rather common strategy used in schools and other organizations. It is a tactic that can enable a principal or manager to just get by, or as is sometimes noted, go along to get along. The strategy behind this tactic is for the manager to let the organization run on automatic pilot, until he or she retires.

This strategy often works well for the individual manager who goes through the accountability steps that satisfy organizational requirements. However, this option has drastic long-term strategic consequences. This is why we have teachers in some schools who should not be in the classroom. Irresponsible supervisors have simply chosen expedient pathways that continue allowing ineffective individuals to continue inferior teaching practices.

This is not, as a number of Republican governors around the country have advocated, due to teacher unions negotiating success. Instead, the fault lies with the moral and ethical failure of weak administrators and school board members who place political connections above their responsibilities for children. These governors' mistaken solution to replace administrator-teacher conversations with more strict accountability management strategies exacerbates the problem. The real problem here is the failure of school board, superintendent, and principal leadership. It is a failure of responsibility that increased accountability cannot fix.

What is hidden is the long-running, consistently ineffective, but often hidden management practice of school administrators who strictly follow the rules of accountability while failing to live up to the moral and ethical responsibility required for leadership. These managers carefully follow evaluation formats and complete forms on time, but the leverage that is available in the process for improving teachers' work is left unused with the excuse that tenure and the unions are to blame.

There have always been processes in place for helping weak teachers improve and removing them when they fail to do so. Probably no public school systems have not required at least two or three years of practice before teachers are granted tenure. This is plenty of time for principals to sort the so-called wheat from the chaff. Additionally, there have always been procedures and processes in place for removing tenured teachers. But the responsible leadership required for this task requires challenge and courage, both elements usually absent from automated modern accountability system designs.

Such leadership requires stepping outside of automatic system management practices. Unfortunately, the new accountability mandates being applied around the country will only add to this problem. The detail devils within the new accountability schemes will burden principals so heavily that these new management tasks will lead to less responsible principal leadership, not more. Additionally, teachers will be less inclined to address individual student needs that vary from increasingly strict curriculum mandates. This is just one more modern solution that regenerates and multiplies the problem. More accountability equals less responsibility.

A third decision option is to do as the author did with the teacher who was challenging the non-grade report card plan. He argued with her. Doing so creates a state of nonproductive discussion that may waste a good deal of time but does not change anyone's opinion. Isaacs's (1999a; 1999b) idea of nonproductive discussion was addressed in earlier sections of this text. The author sometimes calls it "defective discussion." It is talk that is intended to generate change but instead builds barriers to change.

None of these three options is likely to result in desirable change. Each one represents a function of modern, power-driven management, but a failure of leadership. Fortunately, there is a fourth option. What a leader can do is to inquire. Thinking is an internal and individual event influenced by but not controlled by external reality. In other words, only you can change your mind, and questioning provides the reflective process that allows you to do so. These questions can be generated internally or they may come from others.

If you believe that another party or parties in a conversation has a right to an opinion, and you should, then what you can do is begin asking questions—open honest questions. These questions are designed to help you understand the other's thinking or position. That is, you must begin by allowing yourself to be exposed to what the other knows and understands. This means that you must be prepared to alter your own thinking. You may discover that the other conversation participant actually has a better idea, a better understanding, or better knowledge than you have. If you are an honest person, you will allow yourself to change your view.

In other words, a leader is open. A leader recognizes the limits of her or his own thinking and is willing to expose her or his ignorance in pursuit of learning. Real leaders are wisdom seekers who realize that they don't know what they think they know. This actually requires a leap of faith, a rather premodern notion. It requires a belief that there is a representation of reality beyond your current state of knowing, but that open thinking may reveal to you—you can learn.

Practicing openness as a leader provides a pathway not only for your understanding but for the understanding of other organization participants as well. Your inquiry helps you understand another's thinking and helps others understand their own thinking. Behavior modeling is the primary mode of learning for babies. They watch what adults do and mimic that behavior. Adults do so as well, but the imitations are more complex. This human biological attribute lies at the heart of the *LTL* triad. Modeling such openness for another individual is an act of leading: it changes your thinking and allows others to change their thinking as well.

When practicing openness, you place your opinions in an examination space that invites other's questions. Doing so encourages others in the conversation to place their opinions/assumptions in that space as well. In essence, you are saying, "Here is my thinking. What do you think?" This is leading. You move and others will follow. You are modeling the pursuit of wisdom. You are placing the possibility of human learning in a higher space than organizational knowledge. You are opening the worm can of requisite variety.

A leader is a learner and openness to learning creates the opening for others to be open to learning. Open, honest questions provide the door through which you ask another if you may enter into her or his thinking. These questions and their answers provide an invitation for sharing the ideas, beliefs, and assumptions that have meaning for the other. Such questions encourage the other's curiosity about the assumptions that have meaning for you. Both the other's meaning and your meaning are displayed side by side as you both look into this mirror of meaning. You see reflections of the other and yourself.

This is the opening in which leadership occurs. This is the pursuit of wisdom. You, the other, or more likely both of you will be altered by this exchange. This is how a learner is a teacher. It is such a simple yet exquisite complexity. *LTL*: A leader who teaches is a learner. A teacher who learns is a leader. A learner who leads is a teacher. *LTL* is the relational paradox defining the core feature of any true learning organization: two or more individuals in a co-influence relationship.

Leading, teaching, and learning have nothing to do with the formal position an individual has in an organization. In any school context the leader might be the principal, a teacher, a parent, a student, or someone who just cares about schooling our young; hopefully, that would be just about everyone. Indeed, a fourth-grade child's reflective statement that "We are OK," after a forest fire initiated the author's thinking that led to this text. But leading, teaching, and learning have everything to do with the questions that are asked.

SOME EDUCATION POLICY QUESTIONS

What are the questions? The author doesn't know your questions. They are yours. However, the author knows the questions he is asking. They are open, honest questions that need to be addressed in a national conversation about education policy and practice.

Some of these questions are

- Are we teaching our young in ways that best prepare them for an unknown future? Are we too focused on trying to prepare them for work in the jobs that are available now? Does the framing of schooling's purpose around economic competition best serve our needs as a nation? What about developing citizens? What about developing individuals, who independently think, learn, invent, and create? Are these goals as important or perhaps more important than training workers?
- How do our education policies and practices contribute to student, teacher, and community learning? Are education policies that attempt to create a nation of accountable workers appropriate? What jobs will be available for these workers? Who will be the responsible agents that generate the new knowledge necessary for creating these jobs?
- Do we know that our content standards and the developing national standards provide the necessary frameworks our children's future will require? If not, what might be some alternative approaches?
- For what types of learning do standardized tests provide appropriate and effective gauges of student learning? How do the data from these tests support learning in a rapidly changing world? Are there additional or alternative kinds of assessment that may be more appropriate and effective?
- Do we need to examine how education policy and practice address the needs of learners related to the accelerating rate of technological and social change? Do we need to examine the nature of learning for our children as they adapt in and with a rapidly changing world? Are we too focused on developing known skills and content knowledge rather than learning how to develop new skills and invent new knowledge?
- Do we want to continue to develop systems of accountability in schools, or should we investigate the nature of responsible agency? Can we devel-

op education policies that enhance responsible moral and ethical practice? What might such policies be?
- Will contemporary teacher development programs in higher education and professional development programs in school districts generate the complex knowledge of teaching and learning that teachers need to enable students to find success in a rapidly changing world?
- Do we need to investigate accountability and responsibility as attributes in all organizations? What purpose(s) do our organizations serve? To what extent do our organizations serve the needs of people? To what extent are people serving the needs of organization? Should people serve the needs of organizations? If so, then accountability systems may be an appropriate device. Or should organizations serve the needs of people? If so, then we need to focus on how to enhance our natural tendencies toward individual and collective responsibility as we participate in organizations.

Most of this text is a detailed explanation of how these questions came to be. It began by noting that we really do have an education problem. However, the standards framework we have developed places limits on the potential of our young. Simply generating higher test scores will not enable us to compete successfully economically with other nations around the globe. Indeed, rather than competing, Americans need to become outstanding international collaborators and provide the leadership our world so desperately needs: leadership that brings people together rather than separates them from one another.

THE REAL EDUCATION PROBLEM

The real "education problem" is a learning problem. This problem extends well beyond our schools. The education problem is the mistaken belief that we have the knowledge needed to solve all of our social, economic, and political dilemmas. As each solution and set of solutions fail, we fault some institution, some group, or some individual, and do not recognize that the real culprit is our own limited thinking.

This problem stems from the unrecognized limits of modernity and the instrumentalist thinking frames upon which it has been built. It helps us feel safe to believe that the answers to our complex dilemmas can be found in applying the knowledge we have today and generating increasingly complicated solution sets. Unfortunately, these increasingly complicated formulas confound the very problems they were designed to solve.

Collectively, we have made the modern world very convoluted, by creating complicated systems with increasing numbers of parts that appear to fit together in very specific ways as we ignore the complexities we are generating. Our future lies in seeking wisdom by developing a better understanding of the hidden complexities within reality. We need to focus on trying to understand the myriad ways that systems can and do fit together.

Our systems, especially our economic systems, have been built on the notion of growth. However, it is mistaken to continue to assume that our problems are merely complicated issues and that the solutions will be found only through applications of increased quantity. Today, most plans for solving problems include the concept of *more*: more machines, more weapons, more power, more energy, more drilling, more pipelines, and more money. We believe that our economy must grow so that we remain the dominant nation on earth. We must build more and consume more. After all, more has always worked for modern America.

But underneath these complicated assumptions related to growth are complex ideas related to the limits of growth. For centuries, growing human systems have been able to exploit the environment and other humans. However, looking at nuclear accidents, oil spills, growing pollution problems, and starvation as a product of fear and greed suggests that it is time to rethink our definition of growth as *more*.

Indeed, there is one more glaring example of how our limited machine metaphor thinking has extended beyond its value for humankind. It is truly an elephant in the American living room: a literal example of our *growth* problem. About a third of Americans are overweight and this number is increasing. This is creating a frightening national health hazard by increasing weight-related diseases. How has this happened? Modern positivistic thinking is the culprit.

Our modern machine metaphor thinking has successfully generated highly efficient fast-food restaurants and companies that produce snacks whose food-testing laboratories focus entirely on improving the appeals of their products to human taste preferences. The goal is not to improve the health and welfare of these corporations' customers, but to increase the sales of products regardless of the human costs. To verify this, just examine the menu board in any fast-food restaurant or walk down a supermarket isle dedicated to snacks. This is clearly an example of the placement of organizational structures in positions that are superior to human beings.

Is the future just an extension of the past? The answer is yes if reality is merely complicated. But the answer to this question is no. Reality is not only complicated; it is also complex, and a feature of this system is hidden in multilayered dimensions that we usually fail to consider and study. More worked well when our nation had a seemingly unlimited frontier available. Indeed, exploiting this frontier became our national policy and mania.

Unfortunately, we are reaching the limits of more. Our planet doesn't have more space, more air, and more water available to support more people and the continued accumulation of wealth. In fact, the past few generations in America have witnessed declining wealth for most of us and a concentration of wealth within small groups of elites. We need to change our thinking: this is our learning problem. Our limited thinking is our real education problem.

As this limited thinking frame has been applied to schools we see more standards, more testing, more regulation, more accountability, and more centralized control. Now, we are even extending standardized testing into kindergarten. Feeling only the need for "more" is not the solution for our education problem. The nature of our problem is not merely quantitative. Thinking only in quantitative terms is a symptom of the limits of modern thinking. Our solutions are more likely found in studying the qualitative aspects of reality where we may see complexities hidden from modern view.

Can we redefine the concept of more away from quantity and more toward quality? Should we move toward thinking of our citizens' success not only in terms of complicated *more*, but also as complex *better*? Is it time for us to seek wisdom by recognizing the limits of our knowledge? We are reaching these limits and our future will be increasingly dependent upon our ability to evolve our growth-framed system into a system that balances the impacts of human presence with the needs of the other systems of our planet.

What needs to grow is our thinking. Consequently, what and how we teach our young is essential. This is our responsibility for them and to the future. Do we work to achieve the standards of what we know now and test to manage their learning to what is known? Or do we recognize our responsibility to teach our young to learn to lead us to new and, hopefully, better ways to survive and thrive on a planet that, for its own survival must change the activities of its inhabitants? Is it our responsibility to teach our young that we don't know what we think we know? Do we grant them responsibility for their future rather than accountability for our present?

DANGEROUS IRONY: SUCCESS AS FAILURE

This text began with a quotation by Vaclav Havel. He suggested that the modern period began in America and that it came to an end when Americans first landed on the moon. He recognized that the United States has been the leading organization on earth for two centuries. It is sadly ironic that fear of losing our international dominance is freezing our ability to learn. Our fear is freezing our ability to change and adapt—the very elements required for our continued success.

We often read and hear people, especially politicians and pundits, use the term "American exceptionalism." Yes, Americans are an exceptional people. Diversity, independence, and individuality are the exceptions representing character attributes for which we are known and in which we have great pride. Indeed, all human social and economic development is closely associated with the ongoing evolution of exceptions: those individuals who did not fit into usual, normal, or typical patterns.

Early human societies were able to develop because some people developed talents as hunters, others as farmers, others as a variety of craftspeople. This evolution has continued over thousands of years. Eventually, we had artists, scientists, doctors, and lawyers. Today we have microbiologists, quantum physicists, sociologists, meteorologists, systems designers, and even stockbrokers.

New fields of study and practice are generated daily. In the United States we came to label this diversity development as American ingenuity—as if we invented it. We did not, but we have become quite good at developing our exceptional talents. The irony is that by creating standardized curriculum and assessment systems that expect each student to learn about the same thing at about the same rate, we are rejecting the notion that has made us great at the same moment that other nations are opting for ingenuity development.

These elements, coupled with our ability to collaborate, that is, to pull together, and our openness to and fascination with new ideas, have enabled us to accomplish greatness. But this unique recipe for success is threatened by the limits imposed by the unintentional egotism and conceit acquired by those who ascend to positions of power. Robert Oppenheimer used the term "technical arrogance" to describe his recognition of the false power presented by knowledge. Such conceit in the political sphere feeds on our fear and renders us helpless.

Our schools, from preschools to universities, have always been the organizations that enable our citizens to acquire the skills and ask the questions needed to challenge us to invent, create, and be better. It is ironic that even though they are still the most successful of our institutions, they are blamed for our nation's failures. They are truly not efficient in modern economic terms and have resisted continuous efforts to make them into factory mechanisms.

However, from the standpoint of ecological and evolutionary efficiency and success, they contain the elements that have ensured American social and economic prosperity. They are incubators of possibility. Our continued success depends on allowing and encouraging the American exceptionalism described by pundits. This exceptionalism is the requisite variety identified by systems scientists that is necessary for our future to emerge. Such exceptionalism is the direction that schools have repeatedly attempted to move toward even before John Dewey's time but have been repeatedly defeated by the limits of modern thinking now posing as accountability.

Yes, a number of our schools are not successful and that number seems to be growing. But schools cannot be managed to success; they can only be led to success. Our schools can't be fixed because they are not just complicated machines. Rather, as are all human systems, they are both complicated and complex. They can continue to evolve and we can help in that process. Indeed, it is our responsibility to help in that process. Consequently, schooling should focus on generating questions as much as answers. This is because questions address the future and answers at best only address the transient present.

A second irony is that the business world is now discovering that successful ventures depend upon maximizing the development of the unique strengths of the individuals that inhabit those organizations. The Gallup organization, for example, has developed a very successful leadership development program based on that single idea (Buckingham and Clifton, 2001; Rath, 2007). However, responsible teachers have focused on developing each student's strengths for more than a century. Our best schools exhibit the *LTL* adaptive framework that serves as the model for developing a successful organization.

These schools are places of invention because they develop the unique talents and abilities of individuals. They have evolved to focus on strengths. Unfortunately, the assumptions of modern thinking and knowing allow fear of the future to limit the opportunities for our children to develop their exceptional and unique talents and abilities. It is time for us to look beyond the possibilities afforded by complicated modern thinking and learn to shift our focus toward learning more about the complexity beyond and within.

Vaclav Havel identified America's role in leading humanity to the postmodern period. Will America continue to lead in this new age? Will America guide the world through the transition from the modern world to the postmodern world? Or will the United States succumb to the trap of narrow and now modern thinking? Can America lead into the unknown, learn to seek wisdom, and teach the world to follow? Or will we settle for the false safety promised by the arrogance of knowing?

Can we bridge the growing abyss between the rational and the spiritual, the internal and the external, and the objective and the subjective identified by Havel in 1994 and increasingly evident since that time? Will we choose a leadership path toward the pursuit of wisdom that requires responsible agency? Can we continue to encourage our schools to lead the way? Does the *lead, teach, learn triad*, the relational framework so common in classrooms, provide our pathway? Can we begin this inquiry?

References

Ansary, T. (2007). *Education at risk: Fallout from a flawed report.* Edutopia. Retrieved from www.edutopia.org/landmark-education-report-nation-risk.

Argyris, C., & Schon, D. (1996). *Organizational learning II: Theory, methods, and practice.* Reading, MA: Addison Wesley.

Ariely, D. (2009). *Predictably irrational: The hidden forces that shape our decisions.* New York: HarperCollins.

Armstrong, T. (2006). *The best schools: How human development research should inform educational practice.* Alexandria, VA: Association for Curriculum Development.

Belenky, M., Bond, L., & Weinstock, J. (1997). *A tradition that has no name: Nurturing the development of people, families, and communities.* New York: Basic Books.

Belenky, M., Clinchy, B., Goldberger, N., & Tarule, J. (1986). *Women's ways of knowing.* New York: Basic Books.

Bellinger, G., Castro, D., & Mills, A. (2004). *Data, information, knowledge, and wisdom.* Systems Thinking. Retrieved from www.systems-thinking.org/dikw/dikw.htm.

Berliner, D., & Biddle, B. (1995). *The manufactured crisis: Myths, frauds, and attacks on America's public schools.* Reading, MA: Addison Wesley.

Bohm, D. (1996). *On dialogue,* edited by L. Nichol. London: Routledge.

Bracey, G. (2004). *Setting the record straight.* Portsmouth, NH: Heinemann.

Bronson, P., & Merryman, A. (2010). *The creativity crisis.* Newsweek, July 10, 2010. Retrieved from www.newsweek.com/2010/07/10/the-creativity-crisis.print.html.

Brown, J. (2005). *The world café: Shaping our future through conversations that matter.* San Francisco: Berrett-Koehler.

Buckingham, M., & Clifton, D. (2001). *Now, discover your strengths.* New York: Free Press.

Burns, James M. (2008). The power and creativity of a transforming vision. In *Business Leadership*, edited by J. Gallos, pp. 305–10. San Francisco: Wiley.

CBS News Video. *Cronkite and the Vietnam War.* Retrieved from www.cbsnews.com/video/watch/?id=2827337n.

Chia, R., & Holt, R. (2007). Wisdom as learned ignorance: Integrating east-west perspectives. In *Handbook of Organizational and Managerial Wisdom*, edited by E. Kessler & J. Bailey. Thousand Oaks, CA: Sage.

Core Standards.org. *Common core state standards initiative.* Retrieved from www.corestandards.org.

Cromwell, S. (2002). Is your school culture toxic or positive? *Education World* 6 (2): 1.

Darling-Hammond, L. (1988). Policy and professionalism. In *Building a professional culture in schools*, edited by A. Lieberman, pp. 55–77. New York: Teachers College Press.

Dewey, J. (1916). *Democracy and education.* New York: Macmillan.

References

Duncan, A. (2010). *Remarks on OECD program.* Department of Education. Retrieved from www.ed.gov/news/speeches/secretary-arne-duncans-remarks-oecds-release-program-international-student-assessment.

Ellinor, L., & Gerard, G. (1998). *Dialogue: Rediscover the transforming power of conversation.* New York: Wiley.

First to the Top website. (2010). Retrieved from www.tn.gov/firsttothetop.

Fullan, M. (2001). *Leading in a culture of change.* San Francisco: Wiley.

———. (2003). *The moral imperative of school leadership.* Thousand Oaks, CA: Corwin.

Fullan, M., & Hargreaves, A. (1996). *What's worth fighting for in your school.* New York: Teachers College Press.

Gilligan, C. (1982). *In a different voice: Psychological theory and women's development.* Cambridge, MA: Harvard University Press.

Gitlin, A., & Price, K. (1992). Teacher empowerment and the development of voice. In *Supervision in transition*, edited by C. Glickman, pp. 61–76. Alexandria, VA: Association for Supervision and Curriculum Development.

Glover, E. (2003). *The listening leader: A principal's use of dialogue and discussion with teachers.* University of New Mexico: Unpublished Dissertation.

———. (2007). Real principals listen. *Educational Leadership* 65 (1): 60–63.

Goals 2000. (1994). H. R. 1804: Goals 2000: Educate America Act. Retrieved from www2.ed.gov/legislation/GOALS2000/TheAct/index.html.

Gov. Rick Scott, Michelle Rhee announce partnership (2011). Associated Press. Retrieved from www.edweek.org/ew/articles/2011/01/06/396315flscotteducation_ap.html?tkn=QZPFL6dk509ILJyGlEKYAAzl0%2FcBg7jTIhgU.

Greenleaf, R. (1977). *Servant leadership: A journey into the nature of legitimate power and greatness.* New York: Paulist.

Hall, G., & Hord, S. (2006). *Implementing change: patterns, principles, and potholes.* Boston: Pearson Education.

Havel, V. (1994). *The need for transcendence in the postmodern world.* National Constitution Center. Retrieved from constitutioncenter.org/libertymedal/recipient_1994_speech.html.

Heylighen, F., & Joslyn, C. (2001). *The law of requisite variety.* Principia Cybernetica Web. Retrieved from pespmc1.vub.ac.be/REQVAR.html.

Hightower, A. (2011). Weighing States' School Performance, Policymaking. *Education Week.* Retrieved from www.edweek.org/ew/articles/2011/01/13/16stateofthestates.h30.html.

Holly, L., Arhar, J., & Kasten, W. (2005). *Action research for teachers.* Upper Saddle River, NJ: Pearson Education.

Houston, P. (2007). Out of the box leadership. In *Out of the box leadership*, edited by P. Houston, A. Blankstein, & R. Cole, pp. 1–11. Thousand Oaks, CA: Corwin.

IBM Global CEO Study. (2010). *Creativity selected as most crucial factor for future success.* Retrieved from www-03.ibm.com/press/us/en/pressrelease/31670.wss.

Interstate School Leaders License Consortium Standards (2008). Retrieved from teal.usu.edu/files/uploads/asc/elps_isllc2008.pdf.

Isaacs, W. (1999a). Dialogic leadership. *The systems thinker* 10 (1). Retrieved from www.thinkingtogether.com/publications/sythink.pdf.

———. (1999b). *Dialogue and the art of thinking together.* New York: Currency.

Jiang, X. (2010). The test Chinese schools still fail: High scores for Shanghai's 15-year-olds are actually a sign of weakness. *Wall Street Journal.* Retrieved from online.wsj.com/article/SB10001424052748703766704576008692493038646.html.

Kelehear, Z. (2006). *The art of leadership.* Lanham, MD: Rowman & Littlefield Education.

Kessler, E., & Bailey, J. (2007) *Handbook of organizational and managerial wisdom*, edited by E. Kessler & James Bailey. Thousand Oaks, CA: Sage.

Kohm, B., & Nance, B. (2007). *Principals who learn.* Alexandria VA: Association for Supervision and Curriculum Development.

Kotter, John P. (1996). *Leading change.* Boston: Harvard Business School Press.

———. (2002). *The heart of change.* Boston: Harvard Business School Press.

Kozol, J. (2005). *The shame of the nation.* New York: Three Rivers.

References

Lambert, L. (1999). *Building leadership capacity in schools.* Alexandria VA: Association for Supervision and Curriculum Development.

———. (2003). *Leadership capacity for lasting school improvement.* Alexandria, VA: Association for Supervision and Curriculum Development.

Lambert, L., Walker, D., Zimmerman, C., Cooper, J., Lambert, M., Gardner, M., & Slack, P. (1995). *The constructivist leader.* New York: Teachers College Press.

Limerick, P. (1987). *The legacy of conquest.* New York: Norton.

Lloyd, B. (2006). *Wisdom and leadership: Linking the past, present and future.* Paper delivered to the World Future Society. Retrieved from www.collectivewisdominitiative.org/papers/lloyd_wisdom.htm.

Marx, G. (2006). *Future focused leadership.* Alexandria, VA: Association for Supervision and Curriculum Development.

Marzano, R. (2005). *School leadership that works: From research to results.* Alexandria, VA: Association for Supervision and Curriculum Development.

Marzano, R., Kendall, J., & Cicchinelli, L. (1998). *What Americans believe students should know: A survey of U.S. adults.* Executive summary. Standards at MCREL. Retrieved from www.mcrel.org/survey/summary.asp.

McNiff, J., & Whitehead, J. (2006). *All you need to know about action research.* Thousand Oaks, CA: Sage.

Moran, M. (2010). *Teacher performance alone does not raise test scores.* Vanderbilt University Center for Performance Incentives. Retrieved from news.vanderbilt.edu/2010/09/teacher-performance-pay.

Morgan, G. (2006). *Images of organization.* Thousand Oaks, CA: Sage.

National Center for Educational Statistics (NCES). (2007–2008). Measure up: Assessment news for elementary schools teachers. *National Assessment of Educational Progress* 7 (5–4). Retrieved from nces.ed.gov/nationsreportcard.

National Commission on Excellence in Education. (1983). *A nation at risk.* U.S. Department of Education. Retrieved from www2.ed.gov/pubs/NatAtRisk/risk.html.

Noah, T. (1998). *Bill Clinton and the meaning of "Is."* Slate.com. Retrieved from www.slate.com/id/1000162.

No Child Left Behind. U.S. Department of Education. (2001). Retrieved from www2.ed.gov/policy/elsec/leg/esea02/index.htm.

Northouse, P. (2010). *Leadership: Theory and practice.* Los Angeles, CA: Sage Publications.

Ohanian, S. (1999). *One size fits few: The folly of educational standards.* Portsmouth, NH: Heinemann.

O'Toole, J. (2008). When Leadership is an organizational trait. In *Business Leadership*, edited by J. Gallos, pp. 305–10. San Francisco: Wiley.

Palmer, P. (1993). *To know as we are known: Education as a spiritual journey.* New York: HarperCollins.

———. (1998). *The courage to teach.* San Francisco: Jossey-Bass.

———. (2004). *A hidden wholeness: The journey toward an undivided life.* San Francisco: Jossey-Bass.

Pink, D. (2009). *Drive: The surprising truth about what motivates us.* New York: Penguin.

PISA (2009). *Programme for international student assessment.* Organisation for Economic Co-operation and Development. Retrieved from www.oecd.org/edu/pisa/2009.

Popham, J. (2001). *The truth about testing.* Alexandria, VA: Association for Supervision and Curriculum Development.

Quinn, Robert. 2005. Moments of greatness: Entering the fundamental state of leadership. In *Business Leadership*, edited by J. Gallos, pp. 142–54. San Francisco: Wiley.

Race to the top. (2010). Department of Education. retrieved from www2.ed.gov/programs/racetothetop/index.html.

Rath, T. (2007). *Strengths finder 2.0.* New York: Gallup.

Ravitch, D. (2011). Bridging the Difference Blog. *Education Week.* Retrieved from blogs.edweek.org/edweek/Bridging-Differences/2011/01/dear_deborah_i_have_been.html.

Reeves, D. (2006). *The learning leader.* Alexandria, VA: Association for Supervision and Curriculum Development.

Rowden, R. (2008). The learning organization and strategic change. In *Organizational Leadership*, edited by J. H. Munro. Dubuque, IA: McGraw-Hill.

Sagor, R. (2000). *Guiding school improvement with action research*. Alexandria VA: Association for Supervision and Curriculum Development.

Schlechty, P. (2002). *Working on the work*. San Francisco: Jossey-Bass.

———. (2011). *Engaging students: The next level of working on the work*. San Francisco: Jossey-Bass.

Schon, D. (2007). *The reflective practitioner*. London: Ashgate.

The school turnaround field guide. (2011). The Wallace Foundation. Retrieved from www.wallacefoundation.org/pages/executive-summary-school-turnaround-field-guide.aspx#introduction.

Schrag, P. (2004). United States: America's orgy of reform. In *Balancing change and tradition in global education reform*, edited by I. Rotberg, pp. 359–93. Lanham, MD: Rowman & Littlefield.

Senge, P. (1990). *The fifth discipline: The art and practice of the learning organization*. New York: Currency Doubleday.

Senge, P., et al. (1999). *The dance of change: The challenges to sustaining momentum in learning organizations*. New York: Doubleday.

Sergiovanni, T. (2007). *Rethinking leadership*. Thousand Oaks, CA: Corwin.

———. (2008). *The principalship: A reflective practice perspective*. Boston: Pearson Education.

Simons, J., Irwin, D., & Drinnien, B. (1987). *Psychology—The search for understanding*. New York: West Publishing.

Slade, S. (2010). *What other countries are really doing in education*. The Answer Sheet. Retrieved from voices.washingtonpost.com/answer-sheet/guest-bloggers/what-other-countries-are-reall.html.

Smith, A. (2009). *The wealth of nations*. New York: Classic House.

Sternberg, R. (1998). Teaching and assessing for successful intelligence. *School Administrator* 55(1): 26.

———. (2004). What is wisdom and how can we develop it? *Annals of the American Academy of Political and Social Science* 591: 163–74. Sage Publications. DOI 10.1177/0002716203260097.

———. (2006). Creativity is a habit. *Education Week*. Retrieved from www.edweek.org.

Tennessee first to the top: Teacher and principal evaluations. Tennessee Department of Education. Retrieved from www.tn.gov/firsttothetop/documents/021511EvaluationOverview_2_SH_2-8-11.pdf.

Tirozzi, G. (2011). Oh, to be in Finland. *NewsLeader*. National Association of Secondary School Principals. Retrieved from www.nassp.org/Content/158/NewLeader-01.11.pdf.

Trowbridge, R. (2005). *The scientific approach to wisdom*. Doctoral dissertation, Union University. Retrieved from www.wisdompage.com/WisdomResearchers/RichardTrowbridge.html.

Tye, B. (2000). *Hard truths: Uncovering the deep structure of schooling*. New York: Teachers College Press.

Vella, J. (1995). *Training through dialogue*. San Francisco: Jossey-Bass.

Wheatley, M. (2006). *Leadership and the new science: Discovering order in a chaotic world*. San Francisco: Berrett-Koehler.

Wilson, D. (2008). *Evolution for everyone*. New York: Bantam Dell.

Zhao, Y. (2009). *Catching up or leading the way: American education in the age of globalization*. Alexandria, VA: Association for Curriculum Development.

Index

academic achievement discourse, 57, 58, 61, 65, 66, 70, 76
accountability: accountability systems, 2, 6, 11, 19, 130, 140, 154, 156, 157; accountable workers, vii, 6, 9, 16, 122, 132, 156; in Belenky framework, 142; fear, v–vi, 140; as limiting, vii, 2, 121, 130, 160; *LTL*, denying, 7; market accountability, 98, 115, 117; as myth, v, vi, 1, 2, 3; as a power term, 120; reform models, 61; responsibility as superior to, 2, 7, 33, 94, 138, 97, 129, 139, 146, 151, 154, 159; standards and, vii, 17, 29, 159; in "Students First" partnership, 113; teachers and, 6, 15, 33, 56, 86, 129, 131, 143, 146, 153; testing increases demanding, 14, 68; yearly accountability directives, 89
Ackoff, Russell, 49–50, 75
action learning, 88, 91–92
action research, 128, 128, 131, 132, 133, 128, 131, 132
Aiken, Wilford, 97
Ariely, Dan, 62, 62–63, 70, 71, 98, 113, 152
Armstrong, Thomas, 57, 66, 67, 70, 147
Ashby, John Ross, 56, 56–57
Aspen Elementary School, 29–31, 34, 35, 38, 143, 143–145, 148

Bailey, J., 41–42

Baker, Keith, 65
Belenky, Mary, 15, 31, 32, 33, 75, 76, 142–143
Bellinger, G., 49, 50, 75, 76
Berliner, David, 63, 64
Biddle, Bruce, 63, 64
Bohm, David, 112
Bond, L., 15, 31, 75
Bracey, Gerald, 63, 147
Bush, George H. W., 73
Bush, George W., 73
buy-in, 86, 86, 120

cabin as metaphor, 42, 43, 46, 47, 101, 135, 136
Canada and high test scores, 107, 109–110, 115
Carter, Jimmy, 104
Castro, D., 49, 50
Cerro Grande forest fire, 21–22, 53
Clinton Bill, 73, 103
Compton, Robert, 57–58, 59–60, 62, 63
Constitution of the United States, 80–81
constructivism: constructive knowing, 32, 75, 76; defined, 102; Developmental Empowerment and, 10; importance in education field, 136; in leadership framework, 16, 18, 37; *LTL* influencing, 17; in play theory, 136; pragmatism compatible with, 42, 45, 74, 135

creativity: academic achievement discourse affecting, 61, 65; business success due to, 108; creative tension, embrace of, 87, 90, 92; education policies thwarting, 55; imaginary play enhancing, 139; motivation and, 60, 70; network leaders as creative, 95; organizational management schemes limiting, 147; standards as limiting, 29, 107, 108–109; as strength of poor and minority students, 70
Cronkite, Walter, 82

Developmental Empowerment (DE): Aspen Elementary School analysis, 143–145, 146; Belenky framework influencing, 15, 32, 75, 143; continuous social evolution, 77; defined, vii, 15; encouraging organization participants, 17; figure illustrating, 143; levels of, 2, 32–33, 146; *LTL* and, vii, 1, 15, 88; principals, applying to, 147; teachers and, 32–33, 35, 38, 143, 143–145, 146; as a way of thinking responsibly, 16
Dewey, John, 17, 74, 97, 109, 136, 160
disempowered women, 15, 31–32, 75, 142, 143
Dulli, Bob, 66–67
Duncan, Arne, 106, 107, 108, 109, 110, 115

education policies: accountability and, 15; education policy questions, 156–157; future focus, 116–117; as limiting, viii, 13, 14, 55; machine-age thinking, 8; standardized measures favoring, 6, 13, 42, 56, 57, 61
existentialism, 45, 45, 46, 47, 52

failing education system: background, 63, 71; fear as limiting progress, vi; lazy teachers blamed for, 110, 114; limited thinking, 3; *LTL* framework as worthy of emulation, 88; market system as culprit, 111; misplaced blame, 11; as a myth, 83–85, 141, 147, 160; *A Nation at Risk* report, 7, 72–74, 106; schools as beacons of hope, 97; schools blamed for other institution failures, 2, 115; as a symptom of the real problem, 9, 13
feedback, 90, 127, 146, 148, 149
Finland, 107, 109, 110, 115, 133
First to the Top, 2, 113–114, 130
frontier thinking, 54, 55, 57, 58, 59, 58, 100, 158

Gemeinschaft, 98
Gesellschaft, 98
Gilligan, Carol, 75, 76

Havel, Vaclav, 5, 149, 159, 161
hierarchy of needs, 58–59, 70
Houston, Paul, 65, 66, 107, 147
human development discourse, 70–71

IBM study, 108
irrationality, 62, 98, 113, 114, 152
Isaacs, W., 33, 34, 121, 122, 124, 126, 154

Jiang Xueqin, 107

Kessler, E., 41–42
Kohlberg, Lawrence, 75
Kozol, Jonathon, 65, 66

Lambert, L., 16, 38, 88
Lankinen, Timo, 109
law of requisite variety, 56–57
leaders, types of: Americans, 157; business sector, 82; government officials, 81, 93; line leaders, 94–95, 96; media, 82; ministry, 82–83; network leaders, 94, 95, 96; positivists, 27, 128, 145, 146; servant leaders, 37, 92, 96; wisdom seekers, 154, 155, 161. *See also* principals
leadership: change, influencing, 88, 126; developmental leadership, 31; dialogic leadership, 33–34, 35; fear addressing, 80, 81; inquiry in the face of failure, 154; leadership work as cultural work, 120; *LTL* and, 1, 7, 17, 71, 77, 86, 93, 99, 134; open inquiry, 15, 16, 89, 127; openness, practice of, 93, 154–155; opinions, being careful in expressing, 124; power differentials, dealing with, 124; responsibility, 16, 124, 153–154;

schools as worthy of emulation, 19, 83, 84, 84–85; shared leadership, 91, 94
lead-teach-learn triad (*LTL*): changes in thinking as result of, 135; defined, 13, 71, 77; Developmental Empowerment as part of, vii, 1, 15, 88; district and education policies, challenging, 8, 96; empowerment of participants, 90; frailty of knowledge recognizing, 10; as goal of management, 120; good schools exhibiting, 7, 9, 10, 18, 161; inquiry as an action process, 119; leadership in, 1, 7, 17, 71, 77, 86, 93, 99, 134; in learning organizations, vii, 86, 92, 128, 155; open inquiry, vii, 1, 10, 88, 89, 99, 125, 131, 132; responsibility, 16, 17, 86, 132; social evolution providing for, 2, 9, 77, 151; teachers, 7, 10, 14, 91, 132; urgent need for *LTL* practice, 56; wisdom seeking, 9, 17, 18, 42, 51, 74, 77, 125, 134
learning organizations: characteristics of, 86–88; continuous planning, 90, 88, 90, 91; learning from action, 91, 92; *LTL* practice, vii, 86, 92, 128, 155; open inquiry as feature of, 133–134; questioning welcomed, 89, 93; schools as models of, 2, 18, 84, 85, 97, 98, 99, 131; shared leadership within, 94; strategic planning, 85; teachers, 133, 152; type of leaders in, 94, 97
Lee Kwan Yew, 108
Limerick, Patricia Belson, 53–54
Lloyd, B., 50, 51, 52, 76
Los Alamos, NM, 21, 22, 23, 29

machine as metaphor: cause and effect relationships, 6; inappropriate representation of reality, 1, 5, 6; machine image as a myth, 8; obesity problem related to, 158; principals as central machine operators, 28, 145; schools as complicated machines, 160; schools as factories, 2, 11; scientific management, 60; standardization, vi, 5, 12; strategic planning, 85
market norms, 62, 70, 98, 111, 115, 130
Maslov, Abraham, 58–59, 60, 63, 70
McGuinty, Dalton, 109–110

middle- and upper-class students, 69–70, 73
Mills, A., 49, 50
minority students. *See* poor and minority students
modern positivism. *See* positivism
motivation: carrots and stick, 60, 61, 76, 86, 131, 132; coin-operated, 58, 59, 60, 61, 61, 62, 63, 134; 3.0 motivation system, 59, 61, 63, 70
Muir, John, 53

A Nation at Risk, 7, 72–74, 106
No Child Left Behind, 55, 57, 65, 73, 114
nonproductive discussion, 121, 122, 123, 154. *See also* productive discussion
now and narrow thinking: limits imposed by, 119, 139; market values and market norms favoring, 111, 115; play, denial of, 137, 140; as a positivist thinking trap, 105, 106, 114, 115, 128, 161; the present, 100, 101, 102, 103–105; superficiality of, 112; test scores focus on, 128; unions and lazy teachers, placing blame upon, 110

Obama, Barack, 2, 73, 106, 115
Ohanian, Susan, 66, 67, 147
Omolade, Barbara, 75
open classrooms, 71, 109
open dialogue, 34, 122, 123, 124, 134
open inquiry: characteristics of, 81; focused inquiry, 119–120, 131, 132, 133; inquiry practice, creating, 125–127; leadership and, 15, 16, 89, 127; *LTL* and, vii, 1, 10, 88, 89, 99, 125, 131, 132; participation, encouraging, 17; practiced in the best schools, 88; principals and, 93; responsibility and, 89, 127, 132, 133; shared reality, constructing, 37; as a tool, vii, 1, 2, 10, 15; wisdom seeking through, 77, 127, 134
Oppenheimer, Robert, 22, 23, 53, 160
O'Toole, J., 91

Palmer, Parker, 16, 23, 23, 66, 74, 76, 77, 117, 124
patriotism, 18, 100

phonics, 96–97, 129
Piaget, Jean, 17, 136
Pinchot, Gifford, 53–54
Pink, Daniel, 59–60, 63, 70
play, importance of, 136–137, 137–138, 138–139, 139–140, 147
poor and minority students, 12, 65, 70, 72, 73, 83, 84
Popham, James, 68, 69
positivism: academic achievement discourse as product of, 57, 70, 76; cause and effect thinking, 12, 27–28, 45, 58, 75, 101, 105; creativity limited, 61, 147; disingenuous questioning, 124; education policies influenced by, 42, 56, 63, 112; empirical positivism, 8, 12; facts, placing great faith in, 43–44, 49, 52; feedback loop as missing, 148, 149; fixing schools attempt at, 13; gradual evolution of, 85; incentivizing, advocation of, 130, 130; limitations, 51, 53, 55, 63, 67, 72, 99, 84, 101, 128, 129, 145, 151; nature control of, 38, 43, 54; positivist leaders, 27, 128, 145, 146; positivist-objectivist framework, 30, 66, 74, 75; reality viewed as knowable, 52; scientific objectivity and, 17, 27, 41, 52, 53, 112; shared leadership not valuing, 94; technical arrogance, 53, 55, 57, 58. *See also* now and narrow thinking
postmodernism: complexity recognition of, 50, 51; Havel on, 5, 161; learning and schools, 6, 19; *LTL* and, 42, 71, 93; science and, 48; success for every student as postmodern goal, 11; teachers as inquiry practitioners, 152; U.S. as the Imperial China of postmodern world, 66
pragmatism, 17, 42, 45–46, 47, 48, 53, 74, 135
principals: accountability mandates burdening, 154; barriers generating, 17; continuous planning, 90; creative tension embracing, 87; Developmental Empowerment and, 147; feedback, 146, 148, 149; forcing compliance, 153; inquiry practice creation, 125–128, 134; laissez-faire management, 153; leadership challenges, 90; as managers, 120; mistakes handling, 93; open inquiry and, 16, 93; ownership of new programs, encouraging, 15; power differentials, 122; questioning welcomed, 92–93; responsibility and, 121, 125, 132; role of, 87, 148–149; schools as extensions of principals' beliefs, 28; strategic planning, 86; trust, 92, 125; valuing the knowledge of teachers, 38
productive discussion, 89, 119, 122, 123–124, 125, 134

Quality Counts report, 110

Race to the Top, 2, 55, 73, 113
Ravitch, Diane, 88, 111, 115, 147
Reagan, Ronald/Reagan White House, 7, 11, 72, 106
realism, 42, 43, 45
report cards, 30, 31, 35–36, 37, 152, 154
responsibility: in Belenky framework, 142; collective responsibility, 134, 157, 160; Democratic responsibility, 86; focus on developing, 115, 120, 121; leadership and, 16, 124, 153–154; *LTL* and, 16, 17, 86, 132; open inquiry and, 89, 127, 132, 133; principals and, 121, 125, 132; as professional attribute, 16, 121, 132; responsible agency, vii, 2, 6, 96, 122, 133, 146, 140, 148, 152, 156; social norms and schools, 98, 131; as superior to accountability, 2, 7, 33, 94, 138, 97, 129, 139, 146, 151, 154, 159; surgical team as example, 138, 139; teachers and, 6, 32–33, 35, 38, 95, 117, 129, 133, 130, 161
Rhee, Michelle, 113
Rowden, Robert, 85, 86, 87, 88, 89, 90, 99, 128

Sandia National Laboratories report, 73
Schrag, Peter, 83
scientific objectivism, 8, 17, 27, 41, 43, 52, 53, 112, 43
Scott, Rick, 113
self-actualization, 58, 59, 61, 63, 70

self-knowledge continuum, 142–143; figure illustrating, 143
Senge, Peter, 79, 85, 94, 117, 128, 131
Sergiovanni, T., 16, 94, 95, 98, 120
Shanghai and high test scores, 107, 107, 115
Singapore and high test scores, 66, 107, 108
Smith, Adam, 112, 113
Smokey the Bear, lesson of, 21, 22, 23, 38, 44, 55
social norms, 62, 70, 98, 115, 117, 130, 131, 132
standardization: common core standards, 67, 113; content standards, 30, 31, 156; curriculum standards, vi, 8, 29, 29–31, 56, 57, 61, 64, 65, 66, 106–107, 114, 115, 160; education policies favoring, 6, 13, 42, 56, 57, 61; limited choices, 56, 65; open classroom rejection of, 71; poor and minority education not improving under, 72; "Standardistos", 66
standardized tests: academic achievement discourse, 57, 66; Chinese civil service exam, 64; creativity decline, 108; curriculum issues resulting from, 56, 68; defining school success, 107; differentiation in student response, 68–69; education policy questions, 156; false foundation, 8, 137; gaps in student learning, 132; international standardized test comparisons, 65, 106–107; kindergarten testing, 159; lower learning skills, assessing, 69, 114; market norms pushing education to, 62; Program for International Student Assessment (PISA), 106, 106, 107, 107–108, 109, 112, 115; team teaching success, 95; in Tennessee's *First to the Top*, 113
Sternberg, Robert, 49, 50, 69–70, 76, 105
stewardship of nature, 22, 23, 38, 43, 45, 53–54, 54, 67
strategic planning, 85–86, 128, 129, 131, 132, 133
"Students First" partnership, 113

Taylor Frederick Winslow, 59–60, 63

teachers: accountability, 6, 15, 33, 56, 86, 129, 131, 143, 146, 153; Developmental Empowerment, 32–33, 35, 38, 143, 143–145, 146; good teachers, 7, 38, 91, 94, 95, 114, 117, 129; incentives and salaries, 61, 62, 112–113, 114, 115, 134, 147; incentivizing, 130, 131; lazy teachers, blame put upon, 65, 110, 114; learning organizations, 133, 152; as line leaders, 95, 96; loss of motivation, 146, 154; *LTL* and, 7, 10, 14, 91, 132; as network leaders, 95, 96; as professionals, 9, 34; responsibility, 6, 32–33, 35, 38, 95, 117, 129, 133, 130, 161; sabotaging policies, 97, 129, 146; safety in expressing opinions, 30, 35, 126; standards-based curriculums, dislike of, 29–31; status quo, preferring, 24, 32, 33; strategic planning, 86; teacher development levels, 32–33, 129, 143, 145, 146; team teaching, 95–96; unions, 12, 110, 129, 153, 154; veteran teachers, 25; voices of, 32, 38, 121, 125, 126, 129, 145, 148
technical arrogance, 22, 23, 53, 54, 55, 57, 100, 105, 160
Tennessee Value Added Assessment System, 130–131. *See also* First to the Top
tests and testing: Canada and high test scores, 107, 109–110, 115; Chinese civil service test, 64, 65, 66; criterion-referenced tests, 69; Finland and high test scores, 107, 109, 110, 115; high stakes tests, 64, 68, 69, 115; low test scores, 12, 128; NAEP scores, 111, 112; poor and minority test scores, 65, 73; poverty affecting test scores, 110–111, 112, 114, 116; SAT scores, 73; Shanghai and high test scores, 107, 107, 115; Singapore and high test scores, 66, 107, 108; test-based bonus incentives, 114, 115. *See also* standardized tests
Tönnies, Ferdinand, 98

unproductive defensiveness, 33, 36, 121

Vygotsky, Lev, 17, 136

Watkins, James, 73
The Wealth of Nations (Smith), 112
Weinstock, J., 15, 31, 75
Wilson, David Sloan, 48, 112
wisdom: balance theory of wisdom, 49; competing wisdom frameworks, 50, 51, 51, 76; Eastern wisdom, 76; as elusive, 1, 10; five categories of the mind, as part of, 49, 50, 50, 76; inquiry as vital, 119, 127, 148; leaders as wisdom seekers, 154, 155, 161; *LTL* and, 9, 17, 18, 42, 51, 74, 77, 125, 134; open dialogue enabling, 123; open inquiry, seeking through, 77, 127, 134; positivism limiting study of, 41, 42; present-time, not focusing on, 105; questioning welcomed, 93; quotes on, 38, 39; seeking of 99, 100, 105, 151, 157, 159; values, connected to, 50, 52

Zakaria, Fareed, 65–66, 107
Zhao, Yong, 64, 65, 66, 67, 107, 147

www.ingramcontent.com/pod-product-compliance
Lightning Source LLC
Chambersburg PA
CBHW061837300426
44115CB00013B/2422